AGAINST
WHITE FEMINISM

ALSO BY RAFIA ZAKARIA

The Upstairs Wife

Veil

AGAINST
WHITE FEMINISM

Notes on Disruption

RAFIA ZAKARIA

W. W. NORTON & COMPANY
Independent Publishers Since 1923

Against White Feminism is a work of nonfiction. Certain names and potentially identifying details have been changed.

For information about permission to reproduce selections from this book, write to Permissions, W. W. Norton & Company, Inc., 500 Fifth Avenue, New York, NY 10110

For information about special discounts for bulk purchases, please contact W. W. Norton Special Sales at specialsales@wwnorton.com or 800-233-4830

Manufacturing by LSC Communications, Harrisonburg
Book design by Lisa Buckley Design
Production manager: Lauren Abbate

Library of Congress Cataloging-in-Publication Data

Names: Zakaria, Rafia, 1978– author.
Title: Against white feminism : notes on disruption / Rafia Zakaria.
Description: First edition. | New York, NY : W.W. Norton & Company, [2021] | Includes bibliographical references and index.
Identifiers: LCCN 2021011715 | ISBN 9781324006619 (hardcover) | ISBN 9781324006626 (epub)
Subjects: LCSH: Feminism. | Feminism—Moral and ethical aspects. | Women's rights—Moral and ethical aspects. | Women, white—Civil rights. | Minority women—Civil rights.
Classification: LCC HQ1155 .Z35 2021 | DDC 305.42—dc23
LC record available at https://lccn.loc.gov/2021011715

W. W. Norton & Company, Inc., 500 Fifth Avenue, New York, N.Y. 10110
www.wwnorton.com

W. W. Norton & Company Ltd., 15 Carlisle Street, London W1D 3BS

1 2 3 4 5 6 7 8 9 0

For Rania,
my bright shining star

CONTENTS

Author's Note   ix

INTRODUCTION
At a Wine Bar, a Group of Feminists   1

CHAPTER ONE
In the Beginning, There Were White Women   15

CHAPTER TWO
Is Solidarity a Lie?   32

CHAPTER THREE
The White Savior Industrial Complex and
the Ungrateful Brown Feminist   56

CHAPTER FOUR
White Feminists and Feminist Wars   77

CHAPTER FIVE
Sexual Liberation Is Women's Empowerment   104

CHAPTER SIX
Honor Killings, FGC, and White
Feminist Supremacy   140

CHAPTER SEVEN
"I Built a White Feminist Temple"   168

CHAPTER EIGHT
From Deconstruction to Reconstruction   180

CONCLUSION
On Fear and Futures   206

Acknowledgments   211
Notes   213
Index   233

AUTHOR'S NOTE

A white feminist is someone who refuses to consider the role that whiteness and the racial privilege attached to it have played and continue to play in universalizing white feminist concerns, agendas, and beliefs as being those of all of feminism and all of feminists. You do not have to be white to be a white feminist. It is also perfectly possible to be white and feminist and not be a white feminist. The term describes a set of assumptions and behaviors which have been baked into mainstream Western feminism, rather than describing the racial identity of its subjects. At the same time, it is true that most white feminists are indeed white, and that whiteness itself is at the core of white feminism.

A white feminist may be a woman who earnestly salutes the precepts of "intersectionality"—the need for feminism to reflect structural inequalities drawn along the lines of race, faith, class, disability, et cetera, as well as gender—but fails to cede space to the feminists of color who have been ignored, erased, or excluded from the feminist movement. White feminists can attend civil rights marches, have Black, Asian, and Brown friends, and in some cases be Black, Asian, and Brown themselves, and yet be devoted to organizational structures or systems of knowledge that ensure that Black, Asian, and Brown women's experiences, and so their needs and priorities, remain sidelined. More broadly, to be a white feminist you simply have to be a person who accepts the benefits conferred by white supremacy at the expense of people of color, while claiming to support gender equality and solidarity with "all" women.

This book is a critique of whiteness within feminism; it is directed at pointing out what must be excised, what must be broken down, in order for something new, something better, to take its place. It explains why interventions that simply add Black, Asian, or Brown women to existing structures have not worked. Because it is a critique, it has not been possible to present the diversity of views that exist among and between Black, Asian, and Brown women. Others are doing this work, but for that effort to be given its due, this project of dismantling has to be done. This book tackles what "whiteness" has done within the feminist movement; similar work can and needs to be done about how whiteness operates within lesbian, gay, trans and queer movements.

The goal here is not to expel white women from feminism, but to excise *whiteness*, with all its assumptions of privilege and superiority, so as to foster the freedom and empowerment of all women.

AGAINST
WHITE FEMINISM

—

At a Wine Bar, a Group of Feminists

It is a warm fall evening and I am at a Manhattan wine bar with five other women. The mood is warm and cheerful. Two of the women are writers and journalists, like myself, and the other three work in the media or publishing industry. Everyone, except for me, is white. I am excited to have been included this evening, eager to impress and befriend these women I have only known professionally through phone calls and emails.

The first hurdle comes when the waiter comes to take our order. "Let's split a pitcher of Sangria!" someone says, and everyone agrees excitedly; then they turn to me, looking for agreement. "I am on some medications but please, you guys, go ahead, I will drink vicariously through you," I declare with a smile whose wattage aims to cover up all the discomfort, my own and theirs. It is the truth, but I feel ashamed saying it. They know that I am Muslim and I imagine them wondering immediately if I am too uptight to belong among them. "It's not a religious thing," I add once the waiter is gone, "you have no idea how much I would love a glass right now." There is laughter all around the table. Now I worry that the laughter is forced and that this audition for belonging is already over.

The second hurdle arrives a little later, when everyone except me has been softened by Sangria and is exchanging more personal stories, bonding in the way you're supposed to at wine bars in Manhattan on warm fall evenings. I see it coming when one of the women, a noted feminist author, looks at me mischievously. "So Rafia . . . what is your story?" she asks conspiratorially, as if I've been hiding some tantalizing mystery.

"Yeah," one of the others, an editor at a literary journal, chimes in, "how did you even come here . . . like, to America?"

It is a question I detest so much that I learned to deflect it with a stand-up comedy piece. I am performing now, too, but I know the comedy won't do, will seem like too much of a deflection. But I am prepared for this moment, not least because it has proven tricky to navigate so many times before. Often (as I dramatized in the stand-up routine) I offer up a few white lies. I tell people I came to America when I was eighteen to go to college and then stayed.

It is only two-thirds of a lie. The truth is, I came to America as a young bride. One night after dinner, sitting at the edge of my bed in mid-'90s Karachi, I agreed to an arranged marriage. I was seventeen; my husband, thirteen years older and a Pakistani-American doctor, had promised to "allow" me to go to college once we were married. There were other reasons why I said yes, but the possibility of going to college in the United States, something that my conservative family would never allow (or be able to afford), was a major factor. My life until then had been constrained in all sorts of ways, hardly extending beyond the walls that surrounded our home. I had never experienced freedom, so I gladly signed it away.

Arriving in the United States, I moved directly to Nashville, Tennessee. There I attended a Southern Baptist college (when it was still closely affiliated with the Church and where exhortations promising fire and brimstone for all non-Baptists were commonplace), which my new husband had selected and enrolled me in and for which I was to pay via student loans. After graduating college, I begged him for permission to go to law school, to which I had applied, earning a partial scholarship. He refused, then relented, then "changed his mind," reminding me that his marital promise was to let me attend college, *not* law school.

The transactional nature of our relationship glared at me. The next seven years did not change things for the better. During our last fight, the police officer who arrived on the scene took his cue from my suddenly calm and courteous husband and told me to "patch it up." It was only much later that I would learn that this is what police officers tell women who look to them for help, all the time.

I did not "patch it up" but I spent the night clutching my sleeping toddler. The next morning, after my husband left for the hospital to do his morning rounds, I took her, a small suitcase of clothes, a box of toys, and an inflatable mattress, and drove to a domestic-violence shelter, an unmarked and unknown house. A woman with blond hair and bright-blue eye shadow led me there. "Just follow my car," she told me when we met at a Kmart parking lot, and

I did, the *Barney* theme song playing on a loop inside my car to keep my daughter quiet.

I calculate the costs of presenting the abbreviated version of my story to the literary drinks group. Even if I added a few details, the redacted version of the truth could seem curt, closeted. Telling secrets is the material of friendships; I could begin to weave that fabric now, encompassing them in the warp and weft of my story.

But I feel I cannot present the unedited version either. The truth of that ordeal, and what I endured afterward in my struggle to make my own life as a young single mother in the 2000s, seems glaringly inappropriate for the wine bar and my prettily dressed, slightly soused, fashionably woke companions. I have told the whole truth to such women before and the reaction has always been the same. There is the widening of eyes, the look of seriousness and shock, the hands over mouths, the arms slung around my shoulders. When I finish there is genuine sympathy, a fervent digging around in their own imaginations for some similar story, an aunt, a friend, a connection to violence. Then one of two things happens.

If I am lucky, someone makes a joke or suggests a toast and we move on to other topics, which I eagerly take up. More often, when I am not lucky, there is an uncomfortable silence as everyone stares at the table or at their drinks. Then a grabbing of purses and phones and reasons to leave amid declarations of "how good this has been" and "we should do this again" and "thank you for sharing your story." The words are well meant, but the tone is unmistakable. I don't remember ever "doing this again."

I know why. There is a division within feminism that

is not spoken of but that has remained seething beneath the surface for years. It is the division between the women who write and speak feminism and the women who live it, the women who have voice versus the women who have experience, the ones who make the theories and policies and the ones who bear scars and sutures from the fight. While this dichotomy does not always trace racial divides, it is true that, by and large, the women who are paid to write about feminism, lead feminist organizations, and make feminist policy in the Western world are white and upper-middle-class. These are our pundits, our "experts," who know or at least claim to know what feminism means and how it works. On the other side are women of color, working-class women, immigrants, minorities, Indigenous women, trans women, shelter-dwellers—many of whom live feminist lives but rarely get to speak or write about them. There is an inchoate assumption that the really strong women, the "real" feminists, reared by other white feminists, do not end up in abusive situations.

Of course, they do. But a multitude of factors, notably their access to resources, means that they do not usually/ often have to expose themselves by ending up in shelters or in need of public resources. Conversely, women of color, more often immigrant and poor, do have to take help from strangers and the state, they are the visibly needy and the obviously victimized. It is a complex situation; but it fosters/maintains an image of white feminists as the rescuers and women of color as the rescued.

So an inchoate aversion to lived trauma permeates white feminism, which produces in turn a discomfort with and an alienation from women who have experienced it. I've sensed it every time but have only recently been able to attach it to tacit social assumptions around who undergoes trauma. By highlighting Brown and Black and Asian women suffering trauma as the "usual," their victim-hood stemming from their cultures, while suffering white women are portrayed as an aberration, a glitch, white culture, including the feminism that has sprung from it, asserts itself as superior.

It is for this reason that it has been hard for me to own up to the hardships I have endured. Being one of these non-white "others"—and particularly identifying myself as someone who has done time in the trenches, lived in fear of my life, moved from shelter to shelter, and carries the scars of that trauma—will win me momentary praise from white women, I know. And in that moment they will say the right things, marvel at my courage, ask questions about what hiding from an abuser was like, what being a single mother entails. But my ownership of this othered identity will also allow them to demote me mentally below the women who do the real work of feminism, define its boundaries, its intellectual and policy parameters. "Real" feminists, in their eyes, are fighting for the cause in the public arena, untrammeled by the shifting burden of messy experience.

What I feel in these moments is not imposter syn-drome. I know that I have experienced more and overcome more than the women with me tonight. But I also know that my companions' world is split into women of color who have "stories" to tell (or to be told on their behalf) and white women who have power and an inherently feminist outlook. Here lie the mechanics, the levers and pulleys of how Brown and Black and Asian women's experiences are othered, slotted by white feminists under the mental label of "not-applicable to me."

Here, too, "relatability" exerts its cultural tyranny, using the language of personal preference to legitimize the narrowness and rigidity of the collective white imagination. The academic departments, publishing houses, newsrooms, boards of powerful international NGOs, and civil-rights agencies of the Western world are filled with white, middle-class women. In order to be welcomed into these spaces of power, I need to be "relatable" to them, to "fit" into them. And if the spaces are white and middle class (and they are), I must be recognizable in my humanity specifically to white and middle-class people.

On a superficial level, I can demonstrate this kinship via mentions of fervent feminist awakenings in college, dating mishaps on various apps, curated details of an affluent urban life, and diligent skin-care routines. I can also demonstrate it by not mentioning the kinds of experiences that white people believe do not apply to them—certain kinds of domestic abuse, for example, certain kinds of migration, certain kinds of internecine conflict.

The cult of relatability fosters the exclusion of certain kinds of lived experience from the hierarchies of feminist power, with pervasive consequences for feminist thought and praxis. Many institutions involved in feminist policy-making do not just refuse to consider the lived experience of women of color as a useful perspective for colleagues to bring, they actually treat such experience as a strike against applicants, claiming/fearing they will be "less objective" because of it. During my six years of service on the board of directors of Amnesty International USA,

I never once saw any of the many prisoners of conscience whose cases had been highlighted by the organization be invited to participate in policy discussions or be nominated for the board. Even the shelter where I worked had a rule that excluded those who were residents of the shelter from volunteering or working there for an intervening period of several years.

The great lie of relatability is its implied claim that there is one truly neutral perspective, one original starting point, against which all else can be measured. Relatability is subjectivity dressed up as objectivity. The question we're not supposed to ask, when presented with the "problem" of insufficient relatability, is: relatable to whom? And so the stories of women of color are often told but the perspective gained from living such stories never becomes part of the epistemology of feminism.

The functional dichotomy between expertise and experience is in no way incidental. Many white feminists have forged successful careers in punditry and policy on the basis of formal expertise, accumulating qualifications, conducting research, getting published in journals and books. They have staked out a professional space in which ideas can be constructed and dismantled. And because access to educational and professional opportunity is unevenly distributed in favor of white people, this emphasis on expertise becomes a kind of gatekeeping of power that locks out people of color, as well as working-class people, migrants, and many other groups. The introduction of a different kind of authority to this space, then, one founded in lived experiences that these "experts" may not share, is seen as a threat to the legitimacy of their own contribution to women's rights—as if feminist thought and praxis is a zero-sum game, with one kind of knowledge supplanting the other.

This anxiety around the challenge to the primacy of expertise, which goes hand-in-hand with a challenge to whiteness and its hoarding of power, leads to a particular kind of racialized calculus. If an experience or characteristic is associated with a non-white group, then it is coded automatically as valueless, and in turn anyone associated with that experience becomes themselves devalued. This is the way that hegemony protects itself: silencing and punishing difference by stripping away its legitimacy. These kinds of motivated value judgments are at the heart of white supremacy. And this is how white supremacy operates within feminism, with upper-middle-class white women at the top ensuring that the credentials that upper-middle-class white women have remain the most valued criteria within feminism itself.

Sitting at the wine bar, I am aware of all of this. And I can feel my rising anger at having to "keep it light," accommodating the expectations of people unfamiliar with all the things that can and do go wrong for women like me. But a voice deep inside me insists, "You've come so far." I know precisely what it means: I want to have a voice in a way women like me, single mothers, immigrant brides, abuse survivors, women without safety nets or connections or fancy college degrees, rarely get to have. And I almost have it, I tell myself. I'm so nearly there. It's just the difference between being proud of my truth or censoring it.

I choose the latter. "Oh, I was married young and came to college in the U.S.," I say breezily. "He was a jerk," I roll my eyes, "so I divorced him and never looked back." It is just the right amount of information. "Good for you!" one of them gasps. "Wow, I haven't even been married once and you've already been divorced," laughs another from the end of the table. The conversation moves seamlessly on. When the bill comes for the three pitchers of Sangria, it is divided equally among us all. I pay a full share, even though I have nursed a single Diet Coke. Nobody cares to notice.

———

In the gender-only narrative that has dominated mainstream feminism, all women are pitted against all men, against whom they seek parity. In this struggle, however, white women have taken for themselves the right to speak for all women, occasionally allowing a woman of color to speak but only when she can do so in the tone and language of white women, adopting the priorities, causes and arguments of whiteness. But the assumption that women of color and white women all stand at the same disadvantages against men is flawed. All white women enjoy white racial privilege. Women of color are affected not simply by gender inequality but also by racial inequality. A color-blind feminism thus imposes an identity cost on women of color, erasing a central part of their lived experience and their political reality. This makes it impossible to see the ways in which a white-centric feminism is not serving their needs.

Growing up in Pakistan, I saw my mother, my grandmother, and my aunts survive terrible suffering of all sorts. They survived migrations, devastating business losses, inept husbands, lost relations, legal discrimination, and so much more, without ever giving in to despair, without ever abandoning those who relied on them, without ever failing to show up. Their resilience, their sense of responsibility, their empathy, and their capacity for hope are also feminist qualities, but not ones that the current feminist arithmetic will permit. In the value system of white feminism, it is rebellion, rather than resilience, that is seen as the ultimate feminist virtue; my maternal forebears' endurance is labeled thus a pre-feminist impulse, misguided, unenlightened, and unable to deliver change. No attention can be garnered by Pakistani feminists unless they do something that is recognizable within the white feminist sphere of experience—skateboard while wearing their headscarves, march with placards, write a book about sex, run away to the West. The truth that resilience may be just as much a feminist quality as rebellion is lost in the story of feminism written and populated entirely by white women.

This, too, is a legacy of white supremacy: the white gaze has never been disaggregated from feminism itself. It has become the only kind of feminism we recognize or even have language for. And that means that most of the times when women speak "feminism," they unintentionally take on the cadence and color of whiteness.

In my analysis I am deeply indebted to the work of political theorist Gayatri Chakravorty Spivak, whose groundbreaking essay "Can the Sub-Altern Speak?" first pointed out how Europeans assume that they know the other, placing it in the context of the oppressed. Spivak's famous articulation of "white men saving brown women from brown men" has been a theoretical framework that undergirds much of this book.[1] Spivak pointed out how the subaltern could not speak; I am interested in pointing out how the subaltern is now given some chances to speak but is not heard because the foundations of white supremacy (best represented by colonialism and neo-colonialism) have not been dismantled. Unlike Spivak's work, this is not a book of feminist theory but of feminist practice and its problematic genealogies, the problems of the past and the new forms they have taken in our present.

The consequence of being unable to separate whiteness from feminism's agenda is that feminists everywhere continue to be tied to the genealogy and epistemology of white feminists. Black schoolgirls are taught about Susan B. Anthony, unknowingly imbibing reverence for a woman who, annoyed by the progress of the Fifteenth Amendment, told Frederick Douglass, "I will cut off this right arm of mine before I will work or demand the ballot for the Negro and not the woman." South Asian feminists who adore Jane Austen's heroines as models of strength, wit, and judgment are also absorbing Austen's imperialist views, her justifications for white colonizers taking over land without native knowledge. In countless cases like this, the uncritical presentation of white feminism as the definitive and only kind of feminism covertly recruits women of color in its own justification.

There are two antidotes to this.

First, we must excise white supremacy from within feminism. The disproportionate space that has been taken up by whiteness within feminism, and the implicit suggestion that this imbalance exists because only white women are actually feminists, must be repopulated by robust accounts of other feminisms: those that were actively suppressed or erased by colonial domination and white silencing, and those that have been eclipsed in the obliviousness, past and present, of white privilege.

Second, since experience engenders politics, both must be recalibrated into the necessary vocabulary of feminism. The erasure of Black and Brown and Asian women's experiences has meant the erasure of their politics, and both must be urgently revalued as integral to the feminist canon. To make their experience explicit, feminists of all kinds must work to develop their own genealogies, to look at the women in their lives and in their histories who have not been considered "feminist" because they do not mirror the projects and priorities of white women. This work has already been started by the many writers committed to telling the stories of women of color. Voicing and documenting experience is valuable in and of itself, a vital process of affirmation and collective solidarity. But it is also a catalyst to revitalize the political, such that feminism's strategies and goals reach beyond white and middle-class interests to draw in those of all the women whose stories and politics are presently invisible, and whose needs, having been systematically underserved and elided for centuries, are most urgent. Moreover, documentation of experience is also valuable as an affirmation of humanity, solidarity, and collective experience, which are important kinds of self-care for women of color and other marginalized women.

The new story of feminism will be a different story from the one we know today. It is not enough for alternative narratives of women of color simply to exist; they must actually influence the content and the course of the movement for gender parity. And before this can happen, white women must reckon with just how much white privilege has influenced feminist movements and continues to influence the agenda of feminism today. These are not novel suggestions, but they are ones that have been ignored with alarming obstinacy.

I am tired of the pretense of engagement even as the white feminists in power cling to their fear, their filters, the subtle and not-so-subtle ways in which they include and exclude. I want to be able to meet at a wine bar and have an honest conversation about change, about transformation, about how we can bring a failed system down and build a new and better one.

CHAPTER ONE

—

In the Beginning, There Were White Women

In 2007, the much-celebrated feminist playwright Eve Ensler wrote an essay for *Glamour*. "I have just returned from hell," it began, going on to detail her visit to the Democratic Republic of Congo, where she had met "girls as young as nine who had been raped by gangs of soldiers." According to its title, the article is about "Women Left for Dead—And the Man Who's Saving Them," but this is not immediately clear.

Even while detailing the anguish of Congolese women, Ensler manages to keep the attention on herself. "How do **I** convey these stories?" she asks. "How do **I** tell you . . .?" "**I** stay for a week at Panzi. Women line up to tell **me** their stories." Having just recounted a horrific story about "Alfonsine," rather than inviting the reader to reflect on that story, she writes: "**I** look at Alfonsine's petite body and imagine the scars beneath her humble white clothes. **I** imagine the reconstructed flesh, the agony she experienced after being shot. **I** listen carefully. **I** cannot detect a drop of bitterness or any desire for revenge. Writing about the surgery that is needed to repair the fistulas suffered by so many women victims, again she centers herself, saying, "I sit in on a typical operation. . . . I am able to see the fistula." And so on.

Her repeated emphasis on what she herself is doing and hearing, rather than on what she sees and hears, strongly suggests that her goal is to show the crucial role that she, a white woman, is playing in the lives of these women. She is eager to enlist the rest of *Glamour*'s readership as well; they can write to the president of Congo, or they can donate to the hospital where the rape victims are being treated and the rehabilitation center where "they will learn to become political leaders," through Ensler's own website.

Ensler's article in *Glamour* demonstrates how the white savior complex intersects with feminism in the twenty-first century. A white woman takes on the task of "speaking for" raped and brutalized "other" women, positioning herself as their rescuer, the conduit through which emancipation must flow. It is also an example of how the plight of "over there" exists as a foil against which the successes of women in the West can be judged. "How lucky we are," readers of Ensler's article are encouraged to conclude, mournfully shaking their heads at the circumstances of women who live in less civilized parts of the world. It is notable that the naming or erasure of the indentities of women of color is entirely at the whim of the white women telling the story. In cases where people should be mentioned by name, say the nurses and other medical staff (but which may draw attention away from the white woman's central role as savior), they are left out; in others, where confidentiality would be helpful, such as not photographing victims like "Nadine," we are told that she has agreed to be photographed if her name is changed.

The 2020 Annual Letter issued by the Bill and Melinda Gates Foundation provides another example of this calculated and deliberate phenomenon, particularly as it relates to the optics of white women benevolently helping Black and Brown people.[1] The first image used in the report sets the tone: it features Melinda Gates bending down to meet the eyes of an unnamed Black woman wearing a mask and lying on a hospital bed. The subject's anonymity is typical of this kind of iconography. We may assume that the name has been omitted to protect the woman's privacy, but the pattern continues. Even when the people of color depicted are appearing in their professional capacity, providing rather than receiving care, where there would be no need for anonymity, their names are left out. Bill and Melinda themselves, the only white people in the photos, are the only people ever named. A visit to the Gugulethu Health Clinic features unnamed Black and Brown "staff." The section on gender opens with Melinda Gates flanked on either side by two unidentified, diminutive Brown Indian women.

So effective is this mode of virtue signaling that it has even caught on as a trend on dating apps. A website called Humanitarians of Tinder is devoted to pictures of valiant and loving and oh-so-adventurous white women (and some men) dishing out hugs, cuddling babies, and partaking in customary "native" dances.[2] The same template used by Ensler and Gates to harvest public approval or drum up financial backing is now reapplied to the task of attracting sexual partners. As ever, the Black and Brown faces are mere props in a white enterprise.

Not just a recent cultural style limited to dating apps, fashion magazines, and billionaire philanthropists, this habit of centering the white woman when talking about the emancipation of women of color has a genealogy. The "white feminist savior complex," rooted deep in epistemology and in history, took shape in the colonial era. In the home countries of white women, nineteenth-century gender roles and enduring male privilege constrained their freedoms significantly. But setting off for the colonies allowed these women a unique kind of escape. In India or Nigeria they had a significant advantage: white privilege. Still subordinate to white men, they were nevertheless considered superior by virtue of race to the colonized "subjects." This superiority automatically granted them greater power and also greater freedom.

———

"I am a person in this country! I am a person," wrote an effusive Gertrude Bell to her parents in March 1902.[3] She was writing from Mount Carmel in Haifa, where she had come to learn Arabic and get away from the unkind tittering of London society. Bell's outburst was revealing. In her thirties and with a penchant for falling for the wrong men (they were either poor or married or dead or all three), or not falling for them at all (she friend-zoned more than one wealthy prospect), she was far too old still to be single. In a society that expected matrimony and motherhood of its women, this rendered her functionally redundant.

Home reminded Gertrude of her failings, the damning deficiency of having tried and failed at landing a husband. In the exotic East, there was plenty of room for London ladies who had aged out of the marriage market, and as Gertrude soon learned, the privileges of empire more than made up for the disadvantages of gender. Indeed, she was a "person" in Jerusalem, because unlike at home, her whiteness placed her above most of the rest of humanity. No Brown man could control or question her as she traipsed the bazaars in her straw hat and white dresses or chastise her for riding a horse like a man.

Bell's example reveals how some of white British women's very first experiences of freedom beyond home and hearth were caught up with the experience of imperial superiority beyond the boundaries of Britain and Europe. Contrary to the customary slow slog of history, Britain's empire had swelled rapidly through the nineteenth century, and British women had become citizens of empire. At a time when white women were still the legal property of their husbands, the opportunity to taste a little of the power that was usually withheld from them was evidently too tantalizing to resist subjugating others. As one woman put it, "it was an escape from the old stereotyped existence whose comfortable, commonplace round we had run till it had become altogether monotonous and humdrum."[4]

Ironically, or perhaps simply staying true to the political pedigree of the family that supported her financially, Bell herself was opposed to women's suffrage; in 1908 she would serve as the honorary secretary of the Anti-Suffrage League.[5] It makes sense that Gertrude was in it for herself, her rugged individualism at odds with any collective effort.

The idea that *all* women were equal to men and could do what she could do made no sense to her at all. Her faith was in her own exceptional nature.

Bell's opposition to suffrage did not much matter, for there were many other women pursuing the suffrage cause, and they, too, would benefit from their racial superiority as they tended to their lesser sisters across the empire. If Bell found in the breadth of Britain's domain a freedom of movement and lifting of gendered constraints, these suffrage campaigners saw in the very existence of colonized native women the availability of a politically expedient moral contrast. The subjugation of women, they argued, could only be the practice of uncivilized cultures like the ones that had been colonized by the British.

In her 1851 essay "The Enfranchisement of Women," Harriet Taylor conjured a picture of the unemancipated woman in the minds of her readers: the "Oriental or Asiatic" woman who was kept in seclusion and was hence "servile-minded."[6] Later suffragists went much further; one pamphlet from 1879 argued that "if the physical health of a woman is admittedly impaired owing to confinement in a limited space, her mental health also suffers through legislative disabilities . . . it is unfair to deprive her of political liberty and as in the Oriental mode shut her up in four walls."[7] Others used terms like "abject subjection" and "our cruelly crippled sisters in the East" to describe the hapless women they imagined as desperately needing their attention and assistance.

A whole cultural discourse thus highlighted the position of colonized Black and Brown and Asian women within the colonial universe. In the eyes of Victorian society, "Eastern women were doubly inferior being women and Easterners."[8] Even so, white women who traveled to South Asia and the Middle East were very interested in visiting them. Since the female quarters of any wealthy household or palace were known as the zenana, these visits were known as "zenana visits."

Bell herself managed several zenana visits with the famed Eastern women, encounters she records with almost snide condescension in her book *Persian Pictures*. During her first encounter, at the Sultan's palace itself, she finds the conversation lacking despite the efforts of the French interpreter, noting that all their hostess seemed able to manage as a response is "a nervous giggle, turning aside her head and burying it in a pocket handkerchief"[9] The lasting image of the Persian woman as a tittering idiot does not fade despite the appearance of two daughters who speak of their studies in French and Arabic. By the end of it all, Gertrude has determined everything, even the snacks served (lemon ices), to be unsatisfactory. Ever glad to be white and English, Gertrude and her friend take leave of the three ladies who stand gazing after them from the canvas walls. "Their prisoned existence seemed to us a poor mockery of life as we cantered homewards up the damp valley." The sun, Gertrude notes contentedly, has dropped below the horizon in Persia, "bearing the fullness of its light to the Western world—to our own world."

The "zenana visit," was already very much in fashion throughout the eighteenth century, when the first colonists and occasionally their wives set out for the mysterious "Orient." Their novelty wore out a bit as empire ground on, and they became more commonly a stop on the Western tourist route, but the legacy of those intrusions lived on in the form of nineteenth-century feminist rhetoric situating these other women as their inferiors. Most of the women who wrote pamphlets preaching white women's enfranchisement and certainly most of those that consumed them had never been to the East. It is even more doubtful that they had met any of the women from the harems and seraglios against whom they wished to contrast their own condition. The power of the comparison came not from the truth of any of Eastern women's actual conditions but from the imaginative currency of whiteness and non-whiteness. Believing themselves to be superior, white women argued that they deserved higher status and more freedoms than colonized women. That potent "us" and "them" became an indispensable lever for white women pushing for their own emancipation.

The *Glamour* magazine of the 1860s, *The Englishwoman's Review*, was launched to create a platform for this very argument: that white British women, now the leading ladies of empire, should have lives that were visible, free, and politically meaningful, in contrast to the sequestered, conquered, invisible women of the East. It was impossible, after all, that the lives of British women be defined by constraints and constrictions similar to those faced by the lesser women of the world, who had yet to be civilized.[10]

The question of exactly *how* uncivilized Indian women really were raged on for years in the pages of the magazine. This argument cut both ways: on one hand it appealed to pity and the generosity of rescuers (*See how badly Brown men treat Brown women? White men would never be so barbaric*) and it also made an appeal to white dominance (*Whatever Brown women have, white women must have more and better*). The writers of the *Englishwoman's Review* saw their screeds and essays as the material of the continued ascendancy of feminism in Britain, and themselves as "workers in a women's cause who were making history."[11] Some, like the author Bayle Bernard, thought that the wretched Indian women living the "sunless airless" existence were nevertheless educable and hence redeemable, which is why all Englishwomen inside and outside India should "throw their hearts into the work [of educating them] and determine never to rest until they have raised their sisters to their own level and then may the women of India at last attain a position that is honorable to themselves."[12]

Other articles critiqued the use of words like "primitive" or "uncivilized" about people of color and colonial subjects, though of course even these did not include the actual participation of the women in question. Such women were divested of politics of their own, useful only "when explained, modified and put to feminist use."[13] Just like Eve Ensler and countless other white feminists today, Englishwomen writing in these colonial gazettes sought to speak for the women they were trying to save. Then and now, the virtue of saving women of color entitles white women to bylines, enhancing their reputations and elevating their professional status, with no reference to the irony of this transaction.

Whatever the sincerity of the *Review*'s debates about lifting up Brown sisters, in practice they functioned as a glue that united a vast variety of British women under the imperial umbrella, all of them believing in and projecting the vision of imperialism as a benevolent force. As Ens-ler's bravery in traveling to Congo renders her the altru-istic heroine of her report, so the nineteenth-century Englishwomen who decamped to the colonies proved to all the others who stayed at home that empire was not simply the project of the British *man* but that it belonged to women as well. In this "feminized" imperialism, the duty of the imperial woman was to stand with the men who served the empire in shouldering "the white man's burden." An ad in the *Englishwoman's Review* from Janu-ary 1888 said it all: "An Opening for Women in the Colo-nies" beseeched readers to offer their services to colonial peoples because their plight, particularly that of Indian women, should be a "special and deserving object of fem-inist concern."[14]

The white women who arrived in the colonies to build girls' schools or to train teachers were ill prepared to cope with basic cultural differences—for instance, in clothing. If European feminists are terribly annoyed at Muslim women who insist on covering up their bodies today, they were equally annoyed by the lack of coverings worn by Hindu women then. Annette Akroyd was a British woman who set off for Bengal to build a school (inspired by an encoun-ter almost identical to the one described by Ensler two centuries later as the reason she had made her journey to Congo). She found the sari, as a garment, both "vulgar and Inappropriate" as it left women, in her view, semi-nude. "There must be a decided change to their lower garments," she complained in a letter home after her arrival, "for they cannot go into public with such costumes."[15] Even when she encountered a well-to-do Bengali woman, she likened the way that she dressed and sat to a "savage who had never heard of dignity or modesty."

The white women, ostensibly there to help their colonial sisters reach their potential, were quick to use signifiers like clothing and posture as evidence that Brown women were limited by an innate primitivism and that because of this they were in urgent need of white assistance. Meanwhile, by the mid-nineteenth century, almost fifty years before Gertrude Bell arrived in the colonies, Indian women had already created reform-minded women-only organizations. By the 1870s Indian women were already publishing their own magazines that dealt with women's issues with such gusto that the "Women's Press" emerged in the North Indian province of Maharashtra.[16]

In the 1870s, Indian women such as Pandita Ramabai, Soonderbai Powar, and Krupabai Satthianadhan were translating literary texts from English and other European languages into local languages and were active in speaking against their own subordinate role within society.[17] By 1882, not long after Akroyd's ill-fated trip (she soon gave up on the school and got married instead), there were 2,700 educational institutions for girls in India, with a total of 127,000 students and fifteen training schools for teachers.[18] A couple of years later, in 1886, Swarnakumari Devi began the Ladies' Organization, and she was followed in 1892 by Pandita Ramabai, whose Sharda Sadar was dedicated to the education and employment of women.[19] A decade later, the Hindu Ladies Social and Literary Club held its first meetings under the auspices of Ramabai Ranade. From the 1890s onward Indian women were graduating from Indian colleges and universities and agitating for increased educational opportunities.

And in 1905, around the time that Gertrude Bell was discovering her personhood and her superiority to the silly, cloistered women of the East, Begum Rokeya Sakhawat Hossain, the wife of a Bengali civil servant, penned one of the leading feminist texts of Indian literature in English, "Sultana's Dream"—in which the protagonist is transported to a wondrous world without men, where only women run the show. The story was fiction but it reflected the strategy of "separatism" that Indian women had adopted in their organizations, which did not allow men to hold any of the high offices.[20]

On the odd occasion when a white feminist did come into contact with actual Brown women, the results were almost tragicomic. In one such encounter, the Egyptian feminist writer Huda al-Sha'arawi was approached by a Frenchwoman, Mlle. Marguerite Clement. Clement and her friends wanted to deliver a lecture to aristocratic Egyptian women in Cairo about the Western and Eastern attitudes toward the veil. To ensure that these aristocratic women actually attended the event, Clement asked al-Sha'arawi to find someone older and more important to sponsor it. Through al-Sha'arawi's efforts, Princess Ayn al-Hayat Ahmad was persuaded to fill that role. On the day of the event, however, the princess ran late and the white women in charge of the event decided to begin without the presence of the honored guest, prioritizing the British notion of punctuality over the Eastern values of hospitality on one level and actively asserting the right of the white audience to begin proceedings when it suited them. The princess's eventual arrival with her royal entourage caused a commotion that interrupted Clement's lecture and peeved the Western women, who felt the words of one of their own should not have to compete with the arrival of an Egyptian royal, or rather that notions of white etiquette should be privileged over those of the Egyptian women. Eager consumers of the reviews and periodicals that situated colonized women as their inferiors, these white "feminists" began to criticize al-Sha'arawi, and Egyptian women at large, for not knowing proper etiquette. Al-Sha'arawi, in turn, was upset by this cultural condescension toward the Egyptian women who were present, and toward her personally.[21]

There was an element of white fragility in the encounter as well, where white women could not bear being told to pause proceedings until the royal guest had taken her seat without becoming immediately defensive at the suggestion that they were being disrespectful. Then there is the issue of demanding that whiteness remain central: self-righteous indignation about lateness may appear very reasonable, but punctuality, like all qualities, does not have absolute and universal value. Its importance is culturally coded and points in this case toward asserting the supremacy of the white way of doing things as the correct and only way. In cases that involve a bringing together of disparate groups, then, there is the question of whose norms should be respected, whose baseline adopted by all. This is what is meant by "centering whiteness." And such seemingly trivial impulses signal the direction of much more far-reaching ones, revealing the intentions of one group to make the rules for the other.

In non-Western cultures, important guests are often late, and the other attendees duly wait for them as a mark of respect. This is an alternate etiquette to the Western one, neither inherently more right than the other. But for the white women at the lecture, punctuality—prized by white Western culture, at the nub of Protestant and capitalist values of productivity—could not simply be considered a rule for white and Western people: it must be imposed on everyone else too.

The knee-jerk defensiveness of the British women upon being interrupted by al-Sha'arawi is a telling display of white fragility. It demonstrates the discomfort felt when people of color, seen as inherently inferior or in need of help (despite their material condition and experience), fail to show adequate gratitude to their white saviors, expose the shortcomings of those white people implicitly or explicitly, or point out the reality of their racial privilege. This internal discomfort is weaponized externally in any number of ways: as anger, victimhood, a refusal to cooperate or communicate.

Race and feminism are nowhere more integrally connected than in the fight for women's suffrage. It is possible to even argue that the claims of the suffragists were taken seriously only *because* they existed within and against the more troubling prospects of having to grant citizenship to Black, Brown, and Asian men who had been colonized and, in the case of some parts of the world like the United States, enslaved.

Most British suffragettes made no bones about tying their right to vote to their racial identity as Anglo-Saxons. The archival materials of the age are full of evidence of this noxious truth: the suffragist Charlotte Carmichael Stopes began her account of British women's "historical privilege" by citing the "racial character of our ancestors."[22] Helen Blackburn, who published her own history of the women's suffrage movement, glibly agreed, attributing the early equality of the sexes in Britain to "Anglo-Saxon superiority over all the Indo-Germanic races." Millicent Fawcett, who, like all other British suffragettes, thought that representative government had begun in England, asked the rhetorical question, "Why should she (England) not continue to lead as she has led before?"[23]

As the early twentieth century began and British suffragettes drew closer to winning the vote, they wanted their lesser colonized sisters to engage in a parallel struggle. But the politics of women in the colonies at the time, particularly in India, were geared toward winning freedom from colonial rule. Indian feminists like the poet Sarojini Naidu, among scores of others, adopted Mahatma Gandhi's famous slogan: "India cannot be free until women are free and women cannot be free until India is free." Naidu was a leader in the "Quit India Movement," demanding the British leave, or "quit" her homeland. She and hundreds of other women party members participated in civil disobedience and were arrested and jailed by the British.[24]

Meanwhile, British suffragettes refused to support the fight against colonial domination abroad. Even though at home they were fighting the dominance of men who claimed that women could not govern themselves, they reinforced/joined/parroted/echoed these men when it came to arguing that Indians were incapable of governing themselves. They wanted the Indian suffragist women's movement to look and behave exactly like a mini version of their own struggle, and saw the support of the Indian independence movement as a traitorous abandonment of the women's cause.

While refusing to support Indian women in their political goal of self-rule, British suffragettes insisted that they were allies in the project of getting women the vote in a country where no one, male or female, was free. The words of one Indian woman protesting a conference convened by British women could well have been spoken today: "I disputed the right of the British women to arrange a conference on Indian social evils in London, where all the speakers were British and many of them had never even visited India," said Dhanvanthi Rama Rau. "We (Indian feminists) were already assuming responsibility ourselves and we were sure that we could be more successful than any outsiders, especially those that were ignorant of our culture."[25]

Seeing that the Indian feminists were not playing ball, the white suffragists decided to go about fighting for Indian women's right to vote (but not freedom from colonial subjugation) themselves. In 1917 the "Women's Indian Association" was founded in Southern India, geared toward the specific project of getting the franchise for Indian women. The founders of the organization were mostly white women, even including theosophist Annie Besant.

From the beginning of the organization's existence, the leadership of the committee began to lobby various British parliamentary members. They included a radical Jewish MP, Edwin Montagu, who they hoped would support their proposal for franchise for Indian women. In 1918 the proposal to extend the franchise to Indian women was presented before the Delhi Congress. The proposal passed with support from now Dame Millicent Fawcett.

Ultimately, however, white women could not win the franchise for Brown women from white men. In 1918, Viceroy Lord Chelmsford, along with Edwin Montagu, convened the Southborough Franchise Committee to interview Indian women regarding the feasibility of women's franchise. In 1919, the committee, which had only interviewed women in the provinces of Bengal and Punjab, declared that it had not found support for the vote among Indian women. The reason was obvious. Indian women wanted the vote, but in a country free from colonial subjection to the British. What indeed was the power of a vote in a country enslaved? Indian women knew that once the struggle for independence was won, their own right to vote would come with it, as the Congress Party had promised in 1931 that they would provide all women with the vote when they came to power.[26] When the British finally left India in 1947, both the countries created in their wake (India and Pakistan) granted the vote to women in their constitutions.

—

CHAPTER TWO

Is Solidarity a Lie?

In the winter of 2012, I received an email from a man who at the time taught Middle Eastern politics at the satellite campus of a large Midwestern university. We knew each other because of our circulation on the adjunct circuit of the colleges and schools in the area, and my own students had told me that he was an attentive and thoughtful professor. In the email, he said that some close female friends of his were arranging an informal event that would bring together feminists from different parts of the world for a conversation about women's rights. The idea was to have the event open to the larger public to generate local interest in international issues.

Skeptical of these sorts of well-intentioned but vaguely described events and conversations (and not knowing him particularly well), I ignored the email. I was, in those days, spending my days representing women at a domestic-violence shelter and this took up a good deal of my time. The crisis-based legal assistance I was providing to my clients, most of whom were Black, Brown, and Asian immigrant women, kept me busy with the urgent and pressing issues of immigration and child custody that their cases inevitably involved.

Two days before the event, however, I received a call from a friend of mine. During the call, he urged me to attend, not least because it would also be an opportunity to introduce to the community the work I was doing at the shelter with immigrant women. Reluctantly, I said I would do it.

On the day of the event, I spent my lunch hour jotting down some notes about feminism in Pakistan, the subject I understood I would be speaking on that evening. It was a cold and wet one as I trudged toward the venue, balancing bag and umbrella. As I approached, I could see the building was lit up and the hum of voices wafted out into the night. It appeared to be a well-attended event, which made me feel hopeful about the evening.

When I stepped in, a tall, willowy blonde with her hair in braids asked if she could help me. I introduced myself as "one of the speakers," information that immediately led her to consult a printout, held together, I noticed, with a gold paper clip. "Oh you're Rafia Zakaria," she said, crossing off my name. "You're late!" she exclaimed as she apprehended me again, now with a frown, "and you're not dressed in . . ." The half sentence hung in the air as she searched and failed to find the correct word. "In your native clothes!" she finally said. I stood there shocked by the ease with which she chastised me.

Before I could come up with a response, my blonde handler was back in action, leading me through a maze of tables that were interspersed throughout the room. Everywhere I looked there were white women, all of them flushed from the little cups of "free" wine that their "entrance fee" (of which I had only just learned) had got them.

"Here is your table!" my handler declared after we had waded through the crowd. On a white table were a variety of trinkets that I recognized as tchotchkes sold at various tourist stores in and around the airport in Karachi. Someone had also printed out photographs of various Pakistani landmarks, the kind you would find in tourist guide books, and cute children, and placed them in the middle of the earrings, bangles, key chains, and cell-phone cases. Handwritten on a square piece of paper was *Made in Pakistan*.

While I was woodenly taking all of this in, my handler decided I was the sort of stupid that requires specific instruction. She turned to me and said, "So the idea is that the ladies are milling about and you're to try and engage with them and then tell them about your country and show them these handicrafts which are all for sale." I looked around the room and, indeed, next to each table were Black and Brown women dressed in their "native garb." Next to me was "Nepal" and a little ways off was "Kenya." Some were just standing while others were being assailed with questions from white women who had decided this was what counted for participation.

"What languages do they speak in Kenya?" one yelled out. "When did you get here from your native country?" another probed. It was, all of it, a circus; the white women were the roused and rowdy audience and the Brown and Black women the erstwhile performers.

I stood next to my "table" but not against it as I had been instructed. I could see myself from the vantage point of the white attendee: here was a Brown woman and helping her and her kind was as easy as buying a trinket. If one was feeling particularly generous and humane, one could even chat with her to prove her commitment to diversity. I felt sick.

This was a "global bazaar," where the "natives" from various countries could raise money for some noteworthy cause, orphanages, malnutrition, girls' schooling, or even microloans. Like extensions of the merchandise, the women who had been invited to "speak" would stand obediently by the tchotchkes that commodified their culture.

In the shame-laden minutes that followed, nobody ventured near my table or asked me any questions. This was good. I felt suspended, paralyzed by the anticipatory terror that exists when someone raises their hand to strike you, before the actual sting and burn of the slap itself. I was angry, I was ashamed, I was aghast. I saw the Brown and Black women doing the bidding of my handler and others of her kind.

One of them walked by my table. "Is there a problem?" she asked.

"Yes, there is a problem," I replied curtly. "This is not what I was invited to do. I was told that I was to give a small talk about Pakistan." She stared at me, the look of an elementary school teacher dealing with a problem child. "Well, it actually is; you're supposed to engage people and give a little talk," she cooed. "We wanted it to be a bit informal, you know."

I felt stupid to have said anything at all. Where to begin and how to explain? I became quiet and she walked off. When she was gone, I gathered my purse and my folder of "notes" and walked out into the night to my car. I sat there in the dark for a good half hour and cried.

I can still feel the burning shame I felt that day. The event was degrading because its very arrangement situated Black and Brown women as the beseeching, hungry "others" trying to grab the attentions of white women. Instead of a conversation, it was an enactment of power difference. The Brown and Black women, their stories, their histories, had to be abridged to fit the tiny attention span of white women walking by. Fetishized and in "native dress," they could jockey to be the most colorful, the most alluring, along with the trinkets they were selling. It was, in sum, a spectacle, one in which all stereotypes about Brown or Black women or the cultures they represented were reaffirmed, and conversation was only occasioned by the possibility of a transaction.

———

The idea that Brown, Black, and Asian others are really just flavors for consumption in a wide buffet of countries and cultures laid out for white consumers is rooted in and pervaded by white feminism's earliest exchanges with women of color. Even when white women suffragists were agitating for the recognition of their own personhood, their obliviousness to all "other" women was on display. Unlike their British sisters, the American suffragists did not have an entire empire (yet) in which to perform and celebrate their feminist awakenings or export their suffrage movement. They were, however, quite eager to show off their own "new women," modern and forward-looking, as a beacon to all womanhood everywhere. They got the chance to do just that at the World's Columbian Exposition of 1893 in Chicago, which showcased not just how white American women saw themselves but also how they saw *the rest of the world* in relation to themselves.

The geography of how the World's Fair was laid out was also important, a picture of sorts of the American worldview at the time. On one side was the gleaming, blazing "White City" of the future; in the middle was the Women's Building, crammed with exhibits gathered from white American women all over the United States; and on the opposite side of the fairgrounds from the Women's Building was an avenue called the Midwest Plaisance, which was flanked by "villages" that represented all the countries of the world.

Having such a white fair that excluded American Black people was controversial and deliberate. In 1893 racial tensions were high over the Fifteenth Amendment and the integration of Blacks. In the initial planning months, President Benjamin Harrison appointed a commission of 100 representatives from all over the country, all "almond pure and lily-white," to make decisions about the fair, and they were the ones who decided to call the centerpiece of the Exposition "The White City."[1] The centerpiece of "The White City" was electricity and all the wonders that it could produce. There was an electric tram to carry people around from one part of the large exposition to the other. The first "movie" ever made was on display, a seconds-long instance of a man sneezing, astounding the public with moving pictures. There was even a small moving sidewalk.

The White City was also, quite literally, white. Black people were permitted to *visit*, but of the thousands of exhibits, none were devoted to the achievements that Black Americans had made in the thirty years since slavery had been abolished. The only Black employees of the exposition other than those hired to play African savages or serve as porters were a single army chaplain, a couple of nurses and clerks, and some messengers. In the words of Ida B. Wells and Frederick Douglass, who produced a pamphlet decrying the exclusion of African Americans, "the whole history of the Fair was a record of discrimination against colored peoples."[2]

White women from all around the United States, on the other hand, were celebrated in style. For the first time in U.S. history, there was an expressly designed "Women's Building" highlighting their achievements, so that fairgoers could see that (white) American women were, like the rest of the innovative and dazzling entrepreneurs and engineers of the White City, thoroughly modern.

Assigned to oversee the Women's Building, located at the very edge of the White City, an all-white board of lady managers squabbled over which sort of white women—rich society women or activist suffragists—would run the show. Philanthropist Bertha Palmer, not a suffragist but the wife of a very important and very rich white man, faced off against Phoebe Couzins, a longtime suffragist from poor roots, for leadership of the board.

Bertha Palmer wanted the fair to "shed light on [white women's] economic situation in the world" and believed that while women "should be able to do anything they want, they should not want to do *everything*" but should remain "gentle and womanly."[3] Couzins felt that the Women's Building should highlight the suffragist struggle and be more overtly political. But neither was at all interested in including *Black women* in the conversation, or in having Black American women's achievements reflected in the exhibits they intended to represent the progress American women had made.

The World's Fair represented a microcosm of the American world and within it the Women's' Building was its own microcosm. The many hundreds of exhibits from crafts to paintings to household devices revealed the universe of white American women as they saw themselves. That none of these women, from the politically active Couzins to the philanthropically inclined gentlewoman Palmer, felt that the contributions of Black women were part of the American story reveals just how normalized the invisibility of Black women was. Just like British suffragettes who discussed what was best for colonized Indian or Egyptian or African women without consulting them, white American women remained self-absorbed, oblivious to the erasure of Black women.

Actually not oblivious, but active participants in the project of erasure. Black activists, Ida B. Wells among them, petitioned for representation, or at the very least the inclusion of one token member "whose duty it would be to collect exhibits from the colored women of America," but nothing came of it and the contributions of Black women were not included in the Women's Building or elsewhere.

White women, on the other hand, were celebrated in style. On the roof of the Women's Building was a tea room where white women, tired after traipsing through the exhibition, could get a bite to eat and enjoy the cool breeze with an unobstructed view of the Midway Plaisance.

Running out away from the main body of the Fair like a spare limb, the Midway Plaisance was a narrow, crowded strip intended for entertainment and education. Among its fairground rides and snack sellers were model "villages" representing different countries of the world, with people from those countries shipped in to populate them. At the beginning of each day, all the performers participated in a parade. Dressed in their "native" costumes, they marched up and down the mile-long Midway to entice visitors to their various villages. In the case of the Dahomey village, this meant Black American people hired to act the parts of African "savages," allowed only to beat drums and make unintelligible sounds. Frederick Douglass and other Black activists emphatically criticized the Dahomean exhibit, writing that the Dahomeans were there to exhibit the Negro as a repulsive savage.[4]

The Midway Pleasance also included the "Tower of Beauties," which exhibited "live" women from all around the world doing a provocative "Hoochie-Coochie Dance." In some souvenir books, fair-goers were invited to rank the women of the Plaisance from least to most beautiful. If the Women's Building was about the personal achievements of the respectable white woman, outside its confines the "other" woman was exoticized, objectified, and generalized to a crude type.

Here was the world as white Americans saw it at the turn of the twentieth century, white men at its blazing, electrically lit center, white women protectively ensconced in their own building, celebrating their own limited achievements, and everyone else relegated to the periphery of their manufactured modern world, a flat caricature mostly included for entertainment value. Racism was not surprising in the nineteenth century, but it was unjust and the subject of protest even then. What's shocking was how closely it parallels events today. The "Global Bazaar" event that I had found myself storming out of on a rainy mid-week evening was all too reminiscent of the World's Fair a century before.

The women of color, including me, were not terribly unlike the foreign women doing the Hoochie-Coochie, or situated along the Midwest Plaisance. For us "foreign women" tasked with standing next to tables of tourist wares, as for the Black women and foreign women at the fair, the white feminist Women's Building remains impenetrable, a realm of power and discourse and political action where we are not welcome and our absence has never been missed.

The fair's geography and the centrality of white women as the only women whose achievements were worthy of being noted and commended was a precursor to what was to come. On August 26, 1920, the Nineteenth Amendment was finally passed, granting suffrage to all American women. Its text declared: "The right of citizens to vote shall not be denied or abridged by the United States or by any State on account of sex."[5] The celebrations that took place then, and for many years to come, failed to note that this was not a victory for Black women.[6] While the amendment barred reserving the ballot for men only, poll taxes and a maze of other restrictions based on residency, mental competence, age, and so on were still on the books in several states, specifically aimed at suppressing the Black vote.

In 1920, Mary McLeod Bethune, an American educator,

stateswoman, philanthropist, humanitarian, womanist, and civil-rights activist traveled through her home state of Florida to encourage women to vote, facing tremendous obstacles at every step along the route. The night before Election Day in November 1920, white-robed Klansmen marched into Bethune's girls' school to intimidate the women who had gathered there to get ready to vote, aiming to prevent them from voting even though they had managed to get their names on the voter rolls. Newspapers in Wilmington, Delaware, reported that the numbers of Black women who wanted to register to vote were "unusually large," but they were turned away for their alleged failure to "comply with Constitutional tests" without any specification of what these tests were. The Birmingham Black newspaper *Voice of the People* noted that only half a dozen Black women had been registered to vote because the state had applied the same restrictive rules for voting to colored women that they applied to colored men. Some Black women did vote in 1920, but their numbers were small relative to their white counterparts.[7] Though they had been active campaigners for suffrage from the beginning of the movement, Black women in America did not meaningfully win the right to vote until after the civil-rights movement spearheaded by Martin Luther King Jr. led to the passage of the Voting Rights Act in 1965. The inroads made by that law were undercut in 2013 when the U.S. Supreme Court struck down the act, opening up new avenues for voter suppression, such as the purge of voter rolls, closing polling places, and voter ID laws—all of which were an issue in the 2020 election. It is worth remembering that when the victory of the suffragists is lauded every August, it is mostly white feminists who are being celebrated, with continued centralization of those white feminist icons who had histories of racist views.

———

Even white American feminists who passionately championed civil rights for Black Americans were not generally clearsighted in supporting the political aspirations of their "sisters" around the world (or, for that matter, in understanding the intersectional struggles of Black women at home, but more on that later). In this, they followed Simone de Beauvoir, philosopher and author of the groundbreaking feminist text published in 1949, *The Second Sex*. It is fashionable now to celebrate de Beauvoir as a philosopher in her own right who was responsible for key insights of the existential philosophy for which her longtime partner, Jean-Paul Sartre, took credit, including but not limited to the idea of the "other." Yet her work is also foundational in establishing the white woman as "the" woman, the universal subject of feminism.

De Beauvoir's goal in *The Second Sex* is simply this: to carve out for women the position of the universalizable and generalizable subject so that women could begin to exist in the realm of philosophy. Until then, only white men had occupied the position of the generalizable and universalizable subject for European philosophers.

This in itself is a worthy goal, but in comparing "women" to "others," who include Blacks and Jews, de Beauvoir reveals herself to be thinking of "women" as only white women. From the very introductory pages of *The Second Sex*, de Beauvoir identifies "otherness" as the fundamental category and woman as the ultimate "other" in a way similar to how "the natives of a country see inhabitants of other countries as 'foreigners', Jews are the 'others' for anti-Semites, blacks for racist Americans, indigenous peoples for colonists, proletarians for the propertied classes."[8] In de Beauvoir's view, then, the justifications for inferior conditions of race, class, and caste are not just comparable but rather the same. Stereotypes about the "Jewish character" and the "Black soul" are, in her view, equivalent to stereotypes about the "eternal feminine." In this way, she sees each of these as discrete systems of oppression that could be compared, but did not overlap.

Comparisons of women and Blacks continue throughout the book, but they never meet in, say, the category of "black woman." In one section, de Beauvoir compares anti-Black racism to anti-feminism, saying that antifeminists offer "separate but equal" status to women in the same way that Jim Crow subjects Blacks to extreme forms of discrimination. There are, she says, "deep analogies" between women and Blacks; both must be liberated from the same paternalism and master class that wants to keep them in their place.

In every comparison that de Beauvoir makes between women and Blacks, however, the Blacks are assumed to be American and male and the women are assumed to be white. In *The Second Sex*, she uses the character Bigger Thomas in Richard Wright's *Native Son* to evoke the parallel—but not intersecting—situation of women: "he watches planes pass and knows that because he is black the sky is out of bounds for him. Because she is woman, the girl knows that the sea and the poles, a thousand adventures, a thousand joys are forbidden to her: she is born on the wrong side."[9] It does not seem to occur to her that one could be oppressed by both of these systems, race and gender.

In later portions of the book, de Beauvoir shifts her attention to the uniqueness of women's oppression. Unlike Blacks or Jews, she argues, women cannot trace their oppression back to some historical event. Thus she obscures the sufferings and subjugation of Black and Brown and Jewish women, and again, positions the class of "women" as white and Christian. Categories such as these determine the epistemic foundations, and the focus on women as white excludes women of color from both the philosophical category essentialized here and frames of historical reference. Even as she purports to take on the study of women in history, de Beauvoir elects to focus only on women in the West, and more specifically France, dispensing with the rest of history in a footnote.[10]

Neither is that West-centric footnote the only one in *The Second Sex* that is problematic. In another, she comments that "the history of woman in the East in India and China has been in effect that of a long and unchanging slavery."[11] Was she not aware that two years prior to her book's publication Indian women had managed to overthrow the British Empire and win the franchise? Elsewhere, she explains the particular and special character of gender relations in the modern West. "The more a male becomes individualized and lays claim to individuality," she writes, "the more certainly he will recognize also in his companion a free and individual being. The Oriental, careless of his own fate, is content with a female who is, for him, (an object of pleasure) but the dream of the Occidental once he rises to consciousness of his own uniqueness is to be taken cognizance of by another human being, at once strange and docile."[12]

De Beauvoir's own assumptions about Western consciousness and progress are boosted by her thoughtless reiterations of common stereotypes of her place and time, in which the "Oriental lives in the Orient, a life of Oriental ease, in a state of Oriental despotism and sensuality"; the Orient itself is "separate, eccentric, backward, silently indifferent, femininely penetrable"; and the narrative of human progress unfolds in the West "against the timeless culturally static oriental who never quite rises to the occasion of human freedom and history."[13]

Just as de Beauvoir dismisses Indian women as trapped in perpetual slavery, she constantly uses "slavery" to describe the condition of women, by which we now know meant only white women. Yet through her visits to America and access to libraries, she should have known about the particular horrors faced by Black women who had experienced actual slavery.

There are noxious whiffs here of the same beliefs that British suffragists also held, that white women in being companions to white men, the most evolved of all men, automatically deserve equality and better treatment than the women of savage and uncivilized men.

Today, Simone de Beauvoir has been elevated as a timeless feminist heroine. Yet through her powerful influence, her belief in Western cultural supremacy and essentialization of the white woman as the model of all women became baked into the very epistemology of feminism. Successors like Betty Friedan, author of *The Feminist Mystique*—who called de Beauvoir "an intellectual heroine of our history" and credited her with having "started her on the road" of feminism—have repeated her mistakes.[14] Friedan focused on the anomie ("problem with no name") experienced by white middle-class and upper-class women whose sole focus was on their homes, their children, and their husbands, and like de Beauvoir, Friedan essentialized "women" to mean these women.

In the 1970s, another successor to de Beauvoir, the American radical feminist Kate Millett, tried to do better in forging solidarity with non-Western women. She had given theoretical foundation to what became known as second-wave feminism in a book called *Sexual Politics*, a sharp amalgam of literary criticism and sociological study that dissects the work of three of America's literary and artistic heroes—Norman Mailer, John Ruskin, and Henry Miller—to expose how patriarchy serves as the core organizing principle in American society. One commentator credited her with having "destroyed the authority of the male author."[15]

I loved *Sexual Politics* when I read it decades later (just as I had loved de Beauvoir; I had been hurt when I discovered her Orientalist bigotry). I admired Millett's irreverence and was also attracted to her interest in feminist solidarity, built on the sort of radical questioning that could be built in the book. As author and radical feminist Alix Shulman wrote, the book tried to breed in its readers a healthy "epistemological skepticism," which meant a robust questioning of the foundations of knowledge that produced a certain idea, text, or philosophy.[16] The purpose of the stance was to look at the world without considering any foundational truths as unassailable, or as existing in isolation.

Millett modeled the feminist as standing in opposition to many given truths, comfortable in her reading of the world through a gender lens. Millett's stance of epistemological skepticism toward the literary canon created by white men can also be applied to the collusion of racial privilege and feminist thought. If all women adopted this perspective, I wondered, would it be possible to bring about a true feminist solidarity?

At a time when America was at the cusp of the sexual revolution, Millett argued that sex was not just sex after all. Sex between a man and a woman was a matter of power, and hence of politics. Just as she unraveled the unequal power dynamics in the sexual encounter, so too is "feminist solidarity" a political project that inherently involves conflict and contestation. It cannot be a tasty amalgam of meetings and conferences and photo ops and lectures. Constructing a true feminist solidarity involves exposing and excavating the supremacy of whiteness within feminism today. But even Millett found it harder to subject herself, and the domination of white women within feminism, to the same sort of epistemological skepticism that she applied to the "love"-making scenes in the literature of white men.

A lesbian Socialist feminist who believed in a robust internationalism, Millett decided in 1979 to test her own universalism against the reality of working in solidarity with other women who were feminists but who were not white or American. Idealistic and well-intentioned (like so many other white feminists then and now), Millett was interested in collaborating with other women on a basis of equality and mutual learning, one that was attendant to the power differences that race and nationality and class had dealt. So she decided to travel to Iran.

She knew a little bit about the country; the years and months before she ended up in Iran, Millett had been critical about America's foreign policy, in particular its meddling in Iran, not least its installation of the Shah in a CIA-orchestrated coup. Nonetheless, she seemed a bit unprepared when she arrived in Tehran: "The first sight of them was terrible. Like blackbirds, like death, like fate like everything alien. Foreign, dangerous and unfriendly. There were hundreds of them, specters crowding the barrier, waiting their own. A sea of chadori, the long terrible veil, the full length of it, like a dress descending to the floor, ancient, powerful, annihilating us."[17] These Iranian women hardly seemed suitable for the project of feminist political solidarity that the young Millett, raised as she was on the unrest of the 1960s and the transformations of the 1970s, had come to execute in Iran.

Things improved after Millett and her lover, journalist Sophie Kier, met up with activists from the Committee for Artistic and Intellectual Freedom in Iran, the group that had invited her to participate in their celebration of International Women's Day that March 8, 1979. Most, if not all, were affiliated with the Communist Tudeh Party and had protested the Shah for years. During his regime, the Shah had banned the celebration of International Women's Day, preferring Iranian women to celebrate the day when he had ordered them to remove their veils. So the group had made a point of including veiled women in their program, to underscore that the issue of veiling or not veiling was not the basis of true progressivism and that political freedom was at the center of their leftist populism.

Fervent and idealistic, these activists, who had spent the preceding months protesting in the streets of Tehran, young and chic with a disdain for fear, cast a spell on Millett. Between March 5, when she arrived, and March 8, when she would speak, the days were full of political tumult, marching in the streets, huddling and planning in this or that hotel room or apartment. During this time, Millett appears to have realized that the covering and uncovering of women was part of the political theatre of the revolution and had political significance that was more complicated than she had assumed when she characterized veiled women as predatory birds during her first hour in Iran. While most of the women in CAIFI did not wear the veil, they were insistent on courting women who did, believing that solidarity among *all* women was what ultimately mattered; they knew, too, that in the country's post-Shah future, they could not afford to alienate religiously conservative Iranian women. They wanted to show Iranians as a whole, and Iranian women in particular, that the left and the Tudeh Party stood for political freedom for all women, not the superficial modernity that removing the veil implied.

The idea that veiled women had political identities and feminist views was news to Millett. In her account of the event, she describes the first speaker, who "had four of her sons shot down in the insurrection," not as a predatory bird but rather as adorned in a "beautiful garment," her words those of "a firebrand."[18]

But despite her eagerness and openness to learning and understanding, Millett could not completely shed the "white woman in charge" role that white feminists tend to assume when surrounded by women of color. Nor, more sadly, could she apply the idea of epistemological skepticism she had pioneered to expose the power differentials involved in the heterosexual sexual encounter to the power differential between herself and her Iranian feminist counterparts. Whiteness and Westernness, then as now, confer privilege and power regardless of the consent of those endowed. Often white women play along, pretending these were earned, or that they don't exist. This was evident once Millett came before the foreign press.

From the start, Millett *wanted* Iranian women to engage with the international press *themselves*, but she seemed blind to the possibility that in a country ripped apart by U.S. meddling, the choice *not* to engage the Western press might itself be a legitimate political position held by the female freedom fighters who wanted their anti-American credentials to be clear. These women fighters with whom Millett was so enamored did not share her eagerness to engage with the Western media, and were focused instead on the protests that would transform Iran rather than the narrative being conveyed to the rest of the Western world.

Faced by a Western press eager to treat her as a spokesperson for the Iranian Women's Movement, Millett convinced herself that she was in fact a representative of "the rest of the world" in Iran in that moment, and that changing the narrative on Iranian women was too important to quibble about whether she had the right to serve in such a role. "At this moment I am feminist in a fight they are calling espionage, imperialist provocation or anything they can get away with" she wrote. "If I can tell my side, the truth has a chance, I have a chance, all the women here have a chance to go on."[19] Willy-nilly, a white woman had once again put herself in charge of speaking for women who were not white. Millett had deployed the automatic legitimacy conferred upon her, a white American woman, by other Westerners and put herself in the center of a struggle for freedom and justice that was far beyond her knowledge or experience. Not all Iranian women appreciated this.

Millett had failed to apply her technique of epistemological skepticism and the analysis of who has the power to speak and why, as she allowed her own whiteness and Westernness to impose her own frame of analysis on a situation that was never about her, making it the primary lens through which the Western world saw Iran and Iranian women at that moment.

Gloria Steinem and Simone de Beauvoir had also been invited by CAIFI to participate in the International Women's Day celebrations. Millett took pains in her speech to portray other white and Western feminists as having genuine concern about their sisters in Iran. She began "with greetings from Gloria [Steinem], Robin [Morgan], and Angela Davis." In reality, Millett notes, most of the famous women like Steinem had given her the run-around, ignoring her messages and not returning her calls.

This too-busy-to-call-back attitude of VIP feminists transformed just as soon as the world realized that a revolution was under way in Iran. Suddenly all the feminists, including Steinem, now wanted to get into the action, and Millett had to explain why more white women were not likely to do any good (Steinem's onetime CIA employment may have posed a particular problem) and would divert attention from the Iranian women themselves. Instead, she pleaded for "bread [money] for offices, to start publications," and help with getting articles placed—anything and everything so "they know you're with them." No such practical help ever arrived (except in the shape of a loan by French feminists to pay Millett and Kier's hotel bill). Not long after her phone call with Steinem, Millett herself was deported from Iran.

As an otherwise lesser star in the white feminist firmament, Millett became territorial about Iranian women, now functioning as an expert on what others should do. Within this white feminist conversation, Iranian women are peripheral and Millett's being brave enough to be there first becomes primary. Like most white feminists now and then, she explains her wrongheaded role as spokeswoman as a matter of good intentions. She had wanted to help— even if she had never been able to answer the question: "How do you help? How in the hell do you help?"[20]

At the time of Millett's trip, Kimberlé Crenshaw's landmark paper in which she coined the term "intersectionality," arguing that race and gender should *both* be considered in legal cases involving Black women plaintiffs, was still a decade in the future. Crenshaw's logic, if applied to Millett's trip to Iran, might have suggested that Iranian feminists' religio-cultural identity was just as important in understanding their situation as their gender, and that their political positions were more complex than a visiting white woman might immediately grasp. Millett's tacit assumption that feminism in Iran should follow the same model as Western feminism—including in its strategic use of the media—was a failure at such a multidimensional understanding.

In theory, some white feminists today seem eager for a reckoning with the role of whiteness within feminism. The hesitation, the discomfort, the squirming in seats, and ultimately the turning away comes later, when foundational texts or long-adored heroines become the subject of the reckoning. Epistemological skepticism has the potential to uncover theoretical infirmities, cloaked bigotry, or just blatant racism. It reveals how and why the general term "woman" has, in the Western world, been intentionally deployed to mean "white" women.

Can we take what is useful from de Beauvoir's and Millett's pioneering texts while exposing and excising their underpinnings of white privilege and even bigotry? Or should all white feminists with racist and Western-centric failings be eliminated from the story of feminism? In the reckoning that must take place in order for feminism to represent all women, feminists must question whether excising one or another idea from a heroine's corpus can still permit the remainder to stand. Simone de Beauvoir's work is at the center of many white feminist awakenings, but her erasure of Black women, her dismissal of Brown women, is also embedded in her idea of the "self" and the "other."

The cases of Simone de Beauvoir and Kate Millett reveal the lack of epistemological room there has been in white feminist theory for a true understanding of women who are affected by more than one system of oppression. De Beauvoir undoubtedly recognized both race and gender as systems of oppression, but still imagined that race-based oppression happened to Black men and gender-based oppression happened to white women. And despite her radical leftism, Millett could not, for example, understand why her easy assumption of the role of spokesperson trampled over the possibilities of the very solidarity that she and her white feminist sisters were so eager to achieve. But by bringing together the intellectual tools of Millett's epistemological skepticism and Crenshaw's understanding of intersectionality, can a true feminist solidarity finally be born?

Today, from Art Fairs in Indiana, where dancing African women and Brown henna artists are the entertainment, to feminist seminars in New York City, white feminism is still unquestioningly presented as *the* feminism. If women of color have roles in white feminism, they are cameos, the supporting cast or the targets of pity, grasping for survival, or for a school or a health clinic, rather than whole and complex humans. We are expected to be tellers of sad stories, where we detail how our particularly brutal men, our inherently flawed culture, our singularly draconian religion (but never the actions or inaction of white people) have caused us indescribable pain. For their part, white feminists offer us their precious, and perhaps their righteous indignation at the savagery of our native cultures, which have left us in such a hopeless mess, pitiably but patiently waiting for their interventions (by force or by money) to sort things out.

—

CHAPTER THREE

The White Savior Industrial Complex and the Ungrateful Brown Feminist

For a long time, development professionals, NGOs, and the United Nations have been trying to eradicate woodburning stoves in rural India. In the 1990s, after the Beijing Declaration set out the vague agenda of "equality, development and peace for all," the eradication of woodburning stoves became the focus of feminists, modernization advocates, environmental activists, and a slew of other reformers. Together they set about tackling the task of liberating rural Indian women to participate in a wage-earning economy by giving them a better stove than the one that, according to excavations in the area, had been in use since 1800 BCE. The project would deliver empowerment and cleaner air and would end the depletion of forests. The UN Global Alliance for Clean Stoves promised to distribute 100 million "clean stoves" by 2020. The World Bank amassed a $130 million portfolio from thirteen donor countries for the provision of clean stoves.

But no one asked the women who did the cooking whether they wanted the new stoves, or considered the reasons why, it turned out, they did *not* want them: for one, that collecting fuel wood (which does not involve the cutting down of whole trees or have the environmental impact it was alleged to have) had been for centuries a ritual way in which rural women established and maintained their social bonds. It was in these exchanges that they discussed how to solve problems in their lives, how to overcome the many hardships faced by their communities and share their joys and losses, news of relatives and friends. It was an essential part of women-only socialization in these areas.

Also, many/most of these rural Indian women rejected the idea that the route to empowerment was making themselves available for wage-earning work rather than for the literal tending of their own hearths—the cooking and caring for the household from that central point that they saw as an exercise of power. Adhering to traditional recipes and cooking methods that required the old stoves was a reflection of their commitment to the traditions they saw as sustaining their own and their families' lives.

In its original iterations, empowerment was understood as something notably different from its relative meaninglessness today. In the early 1980s, an Indian feminist named Gita Sen and a group of feminist researchers, activists, and political leaders from the global south got together to form DAWN (Development Alternatives with Women

in a New era). Based in Bangalore, India, this collective
sought to push forward women's voices from the global
south.[1] Then and now, the terms of "international development," or aid disbursements to postcolonial nations, were
predominantly dictated by the global north to the global
south—and included imposing the goals of white, Western feminists upon women who were neither white nor
Western and did not necessarily share their concerns.

In her book *Development Crises and Alternative Visions:
Third World Women's Perspectives*, based on the DAWN
collective's work, Sen acidly writes, "Perhaps because
the Western feminist movement (especially in the U.S.)
gained strength in the late 1960s and the early 1970s,
during which time employment, social services and
income (at least of the white majority) were relatively
insulated from the shocks of the world economy, gaining parity with white men often took center stage for the
mainstream of the movement."[2] Thus enraptured with
the ideal of equality between the sexes in the educational and professional spaces they saw opportunities
to access, white and Western feminists largely ignored
poorer women of color who were making the argument that "equality with men who themselves suffered
employment, low wages, poor work conditions and racism within existing socio-economic structures did not
seem an adequate or worthy goal."[3]

Sen was not arguing for doing away with equality as a
feminist goal altogether as much as noting how the agenda
of feminism, internationally and particularly within aid
and development, was being set by what appealed to
white and middle-class women in the United States and

Europe. So she and the DAWN feminists conceived the "empowerment approach," guided by the understanding that the existing white-led, top-down paradigms of development had not delivered any real change in the condition of women in the global south. Instead, they argued for a bottom-up approach, that grassroots organizations could be the actual "catalysts of women's visions and perspectives" and spearhead the structural changes that were necessary within societies. At the center of DAWN's vision of empowerment was "*political* mobilization" supported by education, and the promotion of development "free of *all* forms of oppression based on sex, class, race or nationality."[4]

Anti-racism and political mobilization were thus crucial to the emerging idea of empowerment from the global south. Sen's and DAWN's work invigorated other feminists from the region to speak out and refine the concept all through the 1980s. Indian researcher and activist Srilatha Batliwala, for instance, defined empowerment as "a process of transforming power relationships between individuals and social groups." Batliwala argued that a feminist stance required skepticism toward all existing forms of power and an avid questioning of the ideologies that justified women's subordination. Sen, Batliwala, and other feminists from the global south differentiated "empowerment" from "power"; the latter was simply a system of domination, the former "a collective political power used by grassroots organizations" to "accomplish things." It was the latter that these feminists were after, a project very different from simply grabbing the wheel of the status quo from men and then steering it themselves.

When DAWN and Sen came up with the idea of empowerment, few development agencies were interested in it. A
good number of them, along with their donor organizations, thought "empowerment" was too radical a concept.
Governments all ignored it, providing it with no support
in their agendas. Also silent were powerful organizations
like the American National Organization of Women. Western feminists at the time, including those in development
or at the helm of other international organizations, were
loath to support "political" projects.

Eventually, however, the term began to gain some
acceptance. In 1994, ten years after the formation of
DAWN, at the International Conference on Population and
Development held in Cairo, Sen's definition of the concept
was accepted and received international recognition on
the UN conference circuit. An even greater victory came
the following year, at the Fourth United Nations Conference on Women in Beijing, with the acceptance of a platform for action that described itself as "an agenda for the
empowerment of women," seeking "women's empowerment and their full participation on the basis of equality in
all spheres of society."[5]

The victory was a double-edged sword for the feminists
who had originally pushed for the empowerment of the
global south. Usage of the term climbed steadily, both in
the world of development and in the discourse of mainstream Western feminism, but its definition became more
and more vague—and more and more disconnected from
the idea of collective political action.

"Development," as it existed in the imaginations of
Western would-be saviors, had no room for political agita-

tion, for that might reduce Western donors' power over the recipients. Short-term aid enhances that power, while salving white consciences but developing alternative political structures might prove incompatible with or even challenge the ways the West has built its wealth. "Empowerment" in its original sense could never be integrated into the "foreign aid" idea of "development." So, even though the feminists of DAWN had argued so fervently against top-down programs that sidelined the perspectives of the women themselves, aid disbursement continued to be donor-determined.

If the clean-stove program avoided looking into culture, subsequent feminist development programs actively demonized culture as the source of the women's backwardness and hardship, using this distraction to avoid any talk of politics altogether. So for example, a program against honor killings in Pakistan condemned the local beliefs that led to honor killings but without providing any capacity-building in education and political discussion in local contexts that would allow women to challenge and change the ideas of toxic masculinity that lay behind them. The result of the long-term funding in this program was that legislative measures against honor killing were successfully passed but subsequent years saw no reduction in the numbers of killings themselves.[6] While the law existed on the books, the failure to bring about social and cultural transformation—of the kind that Sen had envisioned—meant that the crime continued to be perpetuated.

Under the cover of technocratic policy mandates and elaborate monitoring procedures, many development programs actually encourage the depoliticization of issues.[7]

Interviews with female cadres demobilizing during peace talks in Colombia reveals how this plays out: "These NGO's like IOM who were brought in by the Santos Government told us they were neutral. They offered us the opportunity to learn to style hair or makeup. They asked us if we wanted sewing machines."[8] The women had gone as far as to take up arms because they wanted to realize political change and gain political rights. Instead of capitalizing on their political identities, the NGO intervention tried to push them back into gendered and domesticated roles and depoliticize them. Even though the very reason for an NGO presence was political, they saw their role as technocratic, with politics as a nuisance that makes their job harder. In this way political resistance, in Colombia or elsewhere, is "NGO-ized."

———

By 2000–2001, "empowerment" appeared alongside "opportunity" and "security" as the three pillars of the World Bank's program for the fight against poverty—aligning the concept of empowerment with capitalist values of growth and wealth creation (opportunity) and with conservative, antirevolutionary politics (security). By 2006, the World Bank had veered even further away from empowerment's original precepts, coupling it explicitly with economic power and progress: "The global community must renew its attention to women's economic empowerment and increase investment in women. Women will benefit from their economic empowerment so too will men, children and society as a whole, in sum the business case for expanding women's economic opportunities is

becoming evident." Not only did social and political transformation not get any mention, the sole reason for investing in women at all was that it made good business sense.[9]

The World Bank was not alone; in other definitions from this time period of what could now be called
empowerment-lite, such as those used by an alphabet
soup of governmental and nongovernmental aid organizations, the political is dropped altogether, deemed too
radical. Even for those who wanted to give money to the
poor or to women's programs, any overt linkages between
poor women and political mobilization—any hint that the
women might be poor at least in part *because* of politics
that the donors supported or enforced—were too threaten-
ing to their self-conception as benevolent grantors.

Development agencies frequently separated political
empowerment and economic empowerment into separate
budget line items so that there would be little possibility
of a holistic approach that would see the two as interconnected. The split also led to a privileging of a meaning
of empowerment more commonly associated with formal
institutions and individual autonomy. Even with the term
"autonomy," the emphasis was on the economic actor con-
tributing to "growth," in the sense of GDP and profit, and
much less on the qualitative experience of the work or the
unpaid-care economy, and even less on issues of bodily
autonomy.

The years following the UN conference in Beijing also
saw an evolving definition of what constituted value. In the
wake of capitalism's presumed triumph in the Cold War,
"value" has meant the possibility that any woman could go
out and get a job and thus monetize her time. Everyone,

from the development subject whose uplift was being strategized to the white feminists in Geneva or New York who were strategizing it, now had to maximize their value.

Again, the clean-stove project is an example of how Western precepts about what constitutes "real" work seeped into development programs imposed on non-Western cultures. In the eyes of rural Indian women, they were already "working" and their labor was already essential without it becoming a part of the wage economy, where the labor available to them would be in menial, physically punishing jobs such as breaking up rocks at construction sites or in the agricultural fields as farmhands. The promised "empowerment" was not actually in the jobs that women would do but in economic, and hence decision-making, power presumably gained within the household. These women, however, saw that working a menial job outside the home might yield a bit more cash, but it would not compensate for the loss of dominion over the hearth of their home, which they deeply cherished.

The conviction that human value and "empowerment" require participation in the cash economy coincided with the rise of neoliberalism—centering free markets while packaging international economic policy in the glib jargon of social justice. In actual terms it converted, as political theorist Wendy Brown puts it, "homo politicus into homo economicus."

On the aid end of the spectrum, neoliberalism required foreign assistance to gloss over the ugly reality of what free markets were doing in the global south. Rich Western countries funded microloans for women in Bangladesh while Bangladeshi textile manufacturers faced high tariffs if they tried to export their products to the West, and Western clothing companies exploited local female labor with impunity. Similarly, encouraging the inclusion of women in peace negotiations in Nigeria might distract the public from what large transnational oil corporations, with blessings from their allies in Western states, were doing to local populations.

In 2007, Srilatha Batliwala, one of the women who had pushed the inclusion of political and social transformation in the original definition of empowerment, showed how its meaning had become "a technical magic bullet" that referred to things like micro-credit programs. "As a neoliberal tool," Batliwala argues, "empowerment is now conceptualized to subvert the politics that the concept was meant to symbolize."[10] It was still overwhelmingly associated with women, but with a depoliticized, consumerist wave of feminism that had risen through the 1990s and 2000s.

The evolution of "empowerment" into a "fuzzword" could be pinned to numerous motives. Rosalind Eyben and Rebecca Napier-Moore argue the ambiguity "created a normative resonance that makes everyone feel good" and without "revealing which meaning they personally favor." The new "fuzzy" empowerment enabled everyone from the president of the World Bank selling a billion-dollar microcredit program to the feminist collective making beaded necklaces to claim they were furthering the cause of empowerment.

One decade on from the UN's official acceptance of the term, no one in the West, including its leading feminists, seemed to remember that empowerment had been introduced by feminists from the global south. And the idea that empowerment was primarily a Brown feminist political project had been erased from mainstream development work. Empowerment was now tied up with a more individualistic notion of power: synonymous with individual capacity, self-realization, and aspiration. Sen's radical idea of a "liberating empowerment" had become something entirely different—"liberal empowerment," or the maximization of individual economic interests.

———

Rather than "empowering" those on the receiving end of aid programs, the development community tends to envision them as helpless, backward, pre-Enlightenment versions of white Western women, whose social and cultural differences from the West are problems to be solved and whose actual problems can be swiftly dispatched using methods that have been tailored to the needs of white people. If the architects of the clean-stove initiative had consulted the rural Indian women properly, the flaws in its premises would have been immediately apparent. Indians were instrumental to the initiative and implementation of the programs, but these Indians belonged to the urban middle class; women in the cities, seeing themselves as more feminist and modern, were eager to collaborate with international feminist efforts. They, too, were enthusiastic about delivering rural Indian women from what appeared to them to be pure drudgery. Often the assent of this cadre of development workers, already eager to identify with the West and its agenda, permits agencies like the UN and their program directors to tick the box for local consultation.

Meanwhile, the underlying premise was not only that rural Indian women have to be taught empowerment through white programmatic interventions but that they were ignorant and apolitical and had no existing ideas or beliefs of their own regarding their own welfare. There is no centering of the woman to be "empowered" here, just the assumption that help will be given in the form deemed most useful by the white donor, and the poor Brown woman will gratefully accept it.

According to researchers, the commercial forestry industry, the clearing of land for agricultural use, urbanization, and broad changes in ground cover all have a much more significant impact on deforestation than the collection of fuelwood.[11] Neither was there much attention paid to the fact that the new stoves were incompatible with certain recipes that required traditional cooking methods and that had been part of the culture for centuries.

Traditional stoves do pollute, they do create smoky interiors, they do require a lot of labor on the part of the women who use them—who can be subject to breathing issues because of them and who surely have ideas about improving them. Meanwhile, the clean stoves broke down and could not be repaired easily in the village, while the old stoves were made of clay.[12] A solution was needed, but it ought not to have been a white-centric solution that made sense only to white and Western program leaders; it had to be a solution that worked for rural Indian women.

Trickle-down feminism, where a solution developed at the top (meaning, generally, by members of the upper or upper-middle class, usually white) is not intersectional feminism; it is dictatorial feminism. This trickle-down framework fosters initiatives like the Gates Foundation Chicken Program, which aims to provide individual women with a degree of economic autonomy via their chickens, which then, it is assumed, may allow them (somehow) to become politically and socially more autonomous as well. Like the clean-stoves program, such endeavors not only overlook women's complex political and social identities but bring a tunnel-visioned focus on the individual as "entrepreneur" rather than on the capacity of women as a collective to bring about social and political change.

In 2015, the Gates Foundation collaborated with Heifer International to donate 100,000 chickens to individual women in some of the world's poorest countries, estimating that a woman with five chickens could make $1,000 a year from selling the eggs, use the profits to buy more chickens, and hence grow her own business.[13] In a long post about the program on Medium, Melinda Gates opined that "a chicken can mean the difference between a family that survives and a family that thrives." Chickens were also deemed exceptional as a tool for women's empowerment because "men don't think chickens are worth their time," leaving the women to tend them and (with the help of the Gates Foundation) so become empowered. The burgeoning numbers of women chicken entrepreneurs would enable the Gates Foundation to claim that they had directly delivered empowerment to tens of thousands of women.

Yet even while Bill Gates was touting the program's benefits, researchers had already pointed out that there was no evidence that chickens provided long-term economic advancement, let alone the empowerment of half of the population. In Mozambique, where the idea had already been tried out, researchers found that while women could make some money in the short term, they were unable to make the chickens a successful commercial venture because large chicken producers with their economies of scale were able to produce cheaper eggs. This meant the women could make at best $100 a year.[14]

One country, Bolivia, earmarked to receive the chickens, called the Gates initiative "offensive" and declined the offer. Cesar Cocanco, Bolivia's minister for land and rural development, said: "[Gates] does not know Bolivia's reality to think we are living 500 years ago, in the middle of the jungle not knowing how to produce," adding "respectfully he should stop talking about Bolivia and once he knows more, apologize to us."[15] No apology, of course, was forthcoming. Bolivia is a major chicken producer, where commercial chicken growers produce 197 million chickens annually.

Imagine: what if, in the poorest rural and urban parts of the United States, where surely "development" assistance is needed, white feminists created a blanket plan to foster gender equality and empowerment by giving every woman a chicken or a sewing machine or a microloan? It is amazing what you can get away with, in defiance of basic logic about how the modern world works, if you're "helping Africa," or other parts of the global south. White and Western women are seen as participants in complex modern societies; their problems cannot be solved with a single neat gift. Women of color are imagined as existing in a much simpler world, held back from success by very basic issues that have very basic solutions.

The Gates initiative was touted in all its promotional material as a project focusing on families in sub-Saharan Africa (or "Africa poor," as a BBC News headline crisply put it).[16] Similar sorts of programs abound, all focusing on women's relative lack of parity in the developing world. Sometimes, they are funded by the scions of corporations who are looking for some strategic virtue signaling to cover up activities that deplete developing countries of the resources that would actually lift their citizens, women included, out of poverty. At other times, they are promoted by Western governments who want to cover up their strategic interventions—for example, neoliberal plans to expand influence within a certain region. The empowerment of women and girls sounds good to political donors and ordinary voters alike. Yet these sorts of allegedly empowering interventions conveniently delink the current condition of women from colonial histories, global capital expansion, transnational investment, and the continued exploitation of feminine labor.[17] Women, it is assumed, are poor because of their culture or their lack of agency or even feminist consciousness, not ever because colonial plunder depleted resources or because current capitalist investment interests calculate their value based on the lowest wage they can be paid to make T-shirts or jeans. The fact that poor countries like Vietnam or Bangladesh cannot compete at the global level without capitulating to these corporate demands (investors will simply turn elsewhere and exploit the women of some other poor country) is not considered. Neither is any attention paid to the fact all of these forces direct the women away from rather than toward a political consciousness.

Similarly absent is any mention of how military invasions, the securitization of borders, and global financial crises all have often disastrous effects on the welfare of women and girls. But Western aid is often used both as a pretext for war and a means to whitewash its terrible humanitarian costs.

In 2001, shortly after the U.S. invasion of Afghanistan, the U.S. Aid and International Development Agency (USAID) began implementing one of the largest disbursements of development aid in history: a program called PROMOTE. Touted as "the world's biggest program ever designed purely for female empowerment," PROMOTE was intended to help 75,000 Afghan women get jobs, internships, and promotions. They would be given training in conducting advocacy and encouraged to set up civil organizations, gaining the leadership skills necessary for Afghanistan's bright new future. In September 2018, seventeen years later, the *New York Times* published a report that showed how terribly PROMOTE had failed in this mission. It was, in the words of the Special Inspector General for Afghanistan Reconstruction (SIGAR), "a failure and a waste of taxpayer money."[18]

A *lot* of money: the program cost $280 million, most of which, according to the *Times* report, was allotted to administrative costs and payments to U.S. contractors. In an interview given to SIGAR, Rula Ghani, the first lady of Afghanistan, pointed out several problems with the program. The girls selected were too young and politically inexperienced to put their training to any good use. She ended with an exhortation: "Anyone working in development, take the time to sit down with the local population and really listen to them. They know better than anyone what is going on."[19]

Trying perhaps to remain in the good books of USAID administrators (to ensure future aid disbursements), Ghani did not mention the official reports from SIGAR that noted serious flaws in the program, including that the metrics of evaluation were continually adjusted to make the program *look* like a success. In some cases, women who attended a single workshop on women's leadership were counted as having benefited from the program, without any follow-up on how the training had helped their long-term prospects. Elsewhere, metrics of "deliverables" were lowered, such that only 20 women out of 3,000 receiving employment and leadership training would have had to find a job with the Afghan Civil Service for the job-training component of the program to be considered a success. But even that number was not "delivered." In the end, the SIGAR report noted, only 55 women could have been said to have benefited from the program, a far cry from the 75,000 target.

For its part, USAID continued to peddle the premise of success. In its formal response to SIGAR, the agency stubbornly insisted that PROMOTE had: "directly benefited 50,000 Afghan women with the training and support they need to engage in advocacy for women's issues, enter the work force and start their own businesses."

The aid industrial complex is a massive part of the global economy, estimated to be worth more than $130 billion per annum.[20] This is money that is funneled through to governments, aid agencies, transnational NGOs, and the thousands of people that work for them.[21] The leadership of this massive system comprises mostly white and Western development professionals, charged with formulating the programs and policies of how aid will be disbursed. The image of the white Westerner as savior, then, is not only a pervasive stereotype, it is built into the organizational and policy-making architecture of the aid industrial complex.

The aid industrial complex is inherently steeped in a power dynamic that mirrors the racialized wealth differential across the globe, in which those who have systematically extracted and accumulated wealth (historically, through stolen resources and stolen labor) hold structural power over people of color (who have been on the receiving end of this exploitation, and the violence and oppression required to enact it). White and Western charity donors will eagerly donate money for girls' education in Bangladesh for the uplift of women, but they will not give up the cheaply produced "fast fashion" that is sold by major American brands and is based on exploiting women in poor countries. The implied goodness of the charitable act thus works to erase complicity in a global system that is instrumental in enforcing global racial hierarchies.

These racial hierarchies also operate within the aid sector. Most policymakers and program directors in major development NGOs are also white, Western, and paid salaries that are astronomically higher than those paid to locals working for the same NGO and doing the same job.[22] Angela Bruce-Raeburn, regional advocacy director for Africa for the Global Health Advocacy Incubator, in an essay titled "International Development Has a Race Problem," affirms that "inherent in the very concept of aid is race and racism because only in this system can majority white societies with ample resources determine what poor people of color need, how much they need, set

up parameters for the delivery of what they need and of
course create elaborate mechanisms for monitoring how
well they have managed the donated funds to meet their
needs." And, she observes, "'helpers' and 'do-gooders'
arrive in places like Sierra Leone oozing natural confidence and bravado, buttressed by their titles as expatri-
ates holding advanced degrees from elite schools in UK
and the US and earning significantly higher salaries than
their local counterparts."

When women of color do get into programmatic roles,
they continue to face discrimination and are often denied
leadership roles. One African woman described her experience working at the United Nations in Geneva as riven
with racism: "When I was at the UN my skin color got in
the way of my advancement," she wrote, and the good lady
in charge told her that she could not be selected to lead
projects because she "would not be able to command any
respect." At other times she was told to change her tone and
her "strong personality" even as she witnessed her white
male boss yell at people and refer to her female colleagues
using the C-word.[23] A recent staff survey of UN employees
in Geneva backed up these descriptions, with 1 out of 3
workers surveyed saying that they had either experienced
or seen someone else experience racial discrimination.
Fifty-nine percent of the survey respondents said that the
UN was not good at dealing with racial discrimination.[24]
Given all of this, it was a dark moment when, at the start
of the Black Lives Matter protests in response to the death
of George Floyd, the UN secretary general told UN staff in
New York that they were banned from attending. Widespread outcry forced him to reverse his decision.[25]

The result of an absence of women of color in these roles means that there is no one to question the hypocrisy in arrangements whereby those who donate money to maintain the face of white benevolence are routinely undercutting the power of the same women they are purporting to help by investing or leading companies that squeeze the life out of the women workers in poor countries to maximize profit. Feminist theorist Gayatri Spivak identifies the well-worn trope of the "rescue mission," saving Black, Brown, and Asian women and girls (inherently helpless and primitive) from their woe-filled realities while masking histories of oppression perpetuated by exactly those white saviors. Silencing the voices of the women involved and sustaining the operative logic of "white men saving Brown women from Brown men," such advocates of development aid would never consider, for example, supporting women in the garment industry in Bangladesh who are trying to unionize to agitate politically for better working conditions. No large garment corporation has ever committed to using only unionized factories and thus "empowering" these women; instead, they donate to and elevate only those causes that fall along the rescue-mission model.[26]

———

Gita Sen was invited to submit an expert paper for the fall 2019 pre-meeting of the twenty-fifth anniversary of the Fourth World Conference on Women in Beijing—planned for March 2020, but canceled due to COVID-19 concerns. It is a glum document, one in which Sen still was trying to draw attention to "human development" in a world obsessed with "economic growth" while noting that women's rights, social mobilization, and empowerment are confronted by even more retrogressive policies now than twenty-five years ago.[27] "Feminist mobilizing does not take place in a socioeconomic or political vacuum through the volitional intent of women's organizations if the environment and institutions are not supportive," Sen noted. Strategies for progress during such a time have to be "defensive and protective" and focused on alliances.[28]

When she wrote the paper, Sen was no doubt gearing up for the tussle that was expected to take place when the Beijing 25 Conference began in New York in March 2020. A global gag order issued by the Trump administration in the early days of his tenure forbade any NGO receiving money if their work touched on "abortion," and had allied with China and Saudi Arabia to ensure that there would be no mention of reproductive rights in the conference resolutions.[29] Individual economic power was still considered empowering, but bodily autonomy was now deleted from the platform altogether. Making no mention of political transformation at all, "The Political Declaration" drafted by the members of the UN Commission on the Status of Women failed to present any meaningful path forward for the world's women.[30]

—

CHAPTER FOUR

White Feminists and Feminist Wars

"I'm fine," the pale, red-haired Jessica Chastain says as she takes off her full black jumpsuit and face mask. The scene is from Kathryn Bigelow's 2012 film *Zero Dark Thirty*, which despite the seeming banality of the dialogue, says a lot about a new flavor of feminism that has evolved in the white and Western world since 9/11 and the War on Terror. In the film, Chastain plays a CIA "targeter" named Maya who is physically delicate but tough as nails in every other way, which in this particular conversation also means that she is up for torture. In fact, that is what she and her male CIA colleague have been doing inside a makeshift bunker that also serves as a torture chamber. "Let's go back in there," she tells the men after they have rested a minute from the hard toils of inflicting extreme pain on other human beings.

Here, then, is gender equality at its most perverse, a white woman trying her best to show a white man that she has as much of an appetite for cruelty as he does. And the laconic white men appear to approve. "She's a killer," her boss says in her wake as she disappears down a hallway. If this had been an entirely fictional film, all of it could have been discarded as the morbid fantasy of some Hollywood director. As it happens, Maya is based on a very real CIA sleuth, whose identity the agency has never released but to whose gritty greatness many have made pointed allusions. Maya (along with others, also mostly women, CIA sources have said) was responsible for the capture and killing of Osama bin Laden in May 2011. The film *Zero Dark Thirty* may be a souped-up, cinematically slick, and action-packed retelling of what the real Maya managed to do, but it is based on fact. For her now-feted heroism, the real Maya won the Distinguished Intelligence Medal, an honor about which she was happy to boast to all her CIA colleagues through a mass email.[1]

I watched *Zero Dark Thirty* in a nearly full movie theater in Indiana. Jessica Chastain's Maya may have been "fine" in makeshift torture bunkers, but I definitely was not. Beyond the movie theater, the shopping mall was all aglow with holiday decorations and around me, my fellow moviegoers seemed snug in the cozy darkness of the theater and smug in this elevation of white women as the ultimate weapon in crushing Brown terrorists.

The crowd repeatedly cheered, once during a scene that showed a Brown man being waterboarded, another time as Chastain's Maya inched closer to catching the man whom the Americans had been hunting for a long decade, and of course at the end as she is hailed as the heroine who crushed the most evil man in the world. The whole exercise was an elaborate revisiting of glory designed to puff the chests of patriots. The end of the film was never a mystery, America had won, and at least for the purposes of the film, a slight, flame-haired, delicate-featured "killer" had sleuthed and tortured her way to ensuring the obliteration of the most wanted Brown man in the whole world.

I cringed, not just because Maya's search for parity with men extends to trash-talking and torture, or even because she calls Pakistan "a really fucked-up place" within the first few minutes of the film, but because it seemed that I was the only person who saw in *Zero Dark Thirty* an utter perversion of the general project of gender equality.

I cried at the end, because the audience stood up to hand the movie a standing ovation. A few months later, the movie was further regaled at the Oscars. Jessica Chastain won Best Actress. The real and the fictive white women had prevailed, become equal to white men in their capacity to subjugate Brown men.

In *Zero Dark Thirty* (and the trueish story behind it), American feminism—once a movement that existed in opposition to the state, as a critique of its institutions and mores—was recast as one that served the state's interests through any means imaginable. This identification with state interests, and the idea of going out to conquer the world with the same mindset of subjugation and domination possessed by white men, seems to have become a warped feminist goal. Put another way, white women wanted parity with white men at any cost, including by avidly taking on the domination of Black and Brown people. As white feminists have progressed within their societies and begun to occupy increasingly important positions, they are constructing a feminism that uses the lives of

Black and Brown people as arenas in which they can prove their credentials to white men.

In her 2019 book *A Woman's Place: US Counterterrorism Since 9/11*, Joana Cook writes that feminism, particularly in relation to the state, used to be focused on promoting peace and *nonviolence*.[2] Being a feminist used to entail a sense of sisterhood with *all* women, discouraging actions where one woman hurt the life and livelihood of other women. The state was understood as propagating and institutionalizing patriarchal norms, and resisting those (rather than adopting them) was considered a feminist act. But in America's War on Terror, the state had subsumed the struggle for equality within itself, giving white women seeming parity with white men in the opportunity to crush Brown, Muslim men, who had become the ultimate antagonist in the white imagination. Crucially, these white women are allowed to take on the 'unfeminine' characteristics of violence and warfare, which would typically threaten the dominant patriarchy they exist under, but only when they exercise this power over someone even lower than them in the white-supremacist hierarchy—that is, on Brown foreigners. Clearly visible in this trade-off is the kind of conditional, limited power that wealthy, nineteenth-century British women experienced when they ventured overseas to British colonies. In both cases, freedom is a zero-sum game, more for one group (white women) only possible as the reinforcement of less for another (non-white people). It is not just the notion of women being violent that is shocking and antifeminist but the racial dimension that is central to this assumption of greater power by white women.

If white American feminists of the 1960s and the

Vietnam era advocated for an end to war, the new American feminists of the newborn twenty-first century were all about fighting in the war alongside the boys. Warfare, traditionally one of the most starkly gendered activities in human society, was opening its arms to women in even its most gruesome and violent moments, and this was seen as a great step forward for everyone.

The War on Terror, at least in theory, was America's first "feminist" war. It wasn't just CIA analysts who were glorified, it was also female soldiers. The story of Pvt. Jessica Lynch is another example. On March 23, 2003, Lynch, a nineteen-year-old truck driver with a maintenance unit of the U.S. Army, was caught in an ambush and captured by Iraqi forces. Eight other soldiers were killed, and Lynch was taken to a hospital, where, according to the Pentagon, she was mistreated by the Iraqis. The U.S. Special Forces launched a secret mission to rescue Lynch; it was alleged that the first words she said when she was found were "I am an American soldier too."[3]

The rescue was recorded and a five-minute video was released to the media by the Pentagon. Within hours she became a media heroine, her courage was feted all over the news, she appeared on the cover of *Newsweek* against a giant American flag, and she was called a "female Rambo" and an "American hero." It was much later that the heroics of Lynch began to be questioned. The BBC aired a scathing documentary that accused the U.S. government of exaggerating the heroics of her rescue and mistreatment by the Iraqis to bolster public support for the war.[4] Many of these allegations were later proven to be true, but the hero-making the Pentagon set out to do in the immediate aftermath of the rescue was already in play. The female American soldier as heroine in the Iraq war was the image Americans would remember. It was notable that the television film *Saving Jessica Lynch*, aired on NBC in 2003, told the same heroic story that had been challenged by the BBC and others. America wanted a soldier-heroine, and they got one.

I also refer to the war as "feminist" because the propagation of women's rights was front and center as an actual goal. American women were liberated, and now they, along with male service members, would go to Afghanistan to root out the misogynist regime of the Taliban. America, thus, was not a cruel superpower bombing a small and hapless nation but a force for good that would actually help bring gender equality to a war-torn country. The effort to eradicate terror (read: *Islamic* terror, not white nationalist terror, despite the latter's considerably larger tally of dead Americans) was one of providing schools and health clinics and even beauty parlors, assisting in legal reform and the development of domestic-violence shelters, drafting progressive constitutions. The small matter of devastating bombings that left thousands dead and more disabled, forever splintered families, and wrecked livelihoods was a necessary means to that shining feminist end. When a white American woman (such as Chastain's Maya in *Zero Dark Thirty*) did something unimaginably violent or cruel, it was part of the larger noble project of helping Afghanistan or Iraq become countries that valued women just as America valued them.

To fulfill the women's liberation portion of the War on Terror, there were efforts to create Yemeni and Iraqi and

Afghan "Mayas"—women trained in warfare drawn from behind enemy lines and reconstituted as double agents, something unusual if not unprecedented in the Middle East and South Asia. Millions of dollars were spent on counter-terrorism training for women, including at least one elite all-female Yemeni counterterrorism unit and two programs, Sisters of Iraq and Daughters of Fallujah (designed to provide incriminating information on the Brothers of Iraq and the Sons of Fallujah, respectively).[5] These programs were based on the premise that Brown women could be weaponized against the Brown men who were their family and friends—that their intrinsic identification with and loyalty to a Western definition of freedom and feminism would supersede their bonds to their communities. But the irony that some Americans could be bombing one village in the morning while other Americans inaugurated a school in another in the afternoon could not pass unnoticed by Afghan women, on whom the interests and aspirations of white American feminists were inscribed.

The point here is not so much that the Countering Violent Extremism (CVE) programs (the new branding given to anti-terror programs) were a failure but rather the smug white feminist assumption that Afghan women were so disconnected from their fathers, brothers, and husbands (all cruel and barbaric in the American imagination) that they would be happy to serve as spies and intelligence gatherers for the Americans. It is this failure, or refusal, to recognize that Afghan women were inextricably connected to Afghan men, and that bombing the men directly affected the women, that explains the failure of many programs initiated in the region.

The entanglement of the "liberating women" agenda with America's endless and ever-expanding War on Terror gave birth to "securo-feminism," a term described by the scholar Lila Abu-Lughod to indicate the collusion between international women's rights advocates and the global security enterprise referred to as CVE. Securo-feminism holds that fighting against terrorism is in itself a kind of feminism. The national shock and grief around the 9/11 attack located this foreign war in a very different category from any that America had fought before. The threat was not abstract or hypothetical, and it was not happening somewhere far away. It felt tangible, immediate, personal. In his book *Bland Fanatics*, the author and historian Pankaj Mishra recounts just how readily the War on Terror and all of its incipient brutalities were accepted even by the intellectual class, which had traditionally been critical of America's military adventures in the developing world.[6] The particular neo-imperialist flavor of the moment was captured in a bit of triumphal reporting by the *Atlantic*'s Robert Kaplan, who gleefully wrote that "Welcome to Injun Country" was the refrain among American soldiers all over the world, who imagined that their mission was playing cowboy to kill and dominate darker-skinned enemies by any possible means.

But the task of saving Afghan women could put a shinier gloss on the job. As the anthropologist Lila Abu-Lughod points out in her book *Do Muslim Women Need Saving?*, Americans promoted a "liberation lie" that positioned them as the saviors of downtrodden Afghan women.[7] From this superior perch, white liberal feminists imagined gender-based violence as something found only

in faraway lands. Among public commentators and journalists, the "liberation lie" facilitated blindness about both
U.S. foreign policy and the problems women face in the
developing world.

In 2002, a coalition of Western women's organizations
sent an open letter to President George W. Bush, asking
him to "take emergency action to save the lives and secure
the future of Afghan women." Its signatories included
Eleanor Smeal, president of the Feminist Majority Foundation in Virginia, together with other notable feminists
such as Gloria Steinem, Eve Ensler, Meryl Streep, and
Susan Sarandon. U.S. women overwhelmingly support the
war, they noted, because it will "liberate Afghan women
from abuse and oppression."[8] The National Organization
of Women (NOW) put out statements in support of the
war and its allegedly "feminist" objectives. Everyone in the
mainstream American and British establishment, including white feminist heroines like eventual Secretary of State
Hillary Clinton and Secretary of State Madeleine Albright,
signed on wholeheartedly to the cause of fighting the War
on Terror via any means that the military, the CIA, or the
president thought necessary. The disconnect between the
practice of American brutality and preaching of American
saviordom managed to escape notice.

In July 2004, three years into the invasion of Afghanistan, Bush announced victory: "Three years ago, the small-
est displays of joy were outlawed. Women were beaten
for wearing brightly colored shoes. Today, we witness
the rebirth of a vibrant Afghan culture."[9] More recently,
a *New York Times* headline tried to celebrate victory even
while noting that women themselves had a different expe-

rience: "Shelters Have Saved Countless Afghan Women, Then Why Are They Scared?"[10] The article did not note that the "countless" were a fraction of the 32,000 civilians that Americans and Western forces had killed during the occupation.[11]

Thus, a new flavor of white American feminism was born. Bolstered by the history of white supremacy within feminism, it resurrected nationalistic themes and made the international propagation of feminist values, such as gender equality, a necessary component of American feminism itself. Securo-feminism, a term coined by Columbia scholar Lila Abu-Lughod, stands for the collusion between countering violent extremism (CVE) initiatives and global gender rights advocacy. Securo-feminists were not simply invested in fighting the War on Terror, they were also committed to using American military power to promote American values all over the world. Just as imperial feminists during the British colonial era had convinced themselves of their own benevolence in improving the lives of native women, so too did securo-feminists believe that they were "saving" Afghanis and Iraqis from themselves.

The birth of securo-feminism was not an accident or a coincidence. The Bush administration's discourse on the Global War on Terror propagated the notion that belief in women's dignity and women's equality required support for the War on Terror. Yet the history of racial privilege that made white women so comfortable in claiming moral authority and in exercising power over Brown men went largely unexamined.

When Iraq became the second venue after Afghanistan for the great American experiment in democracy promotion, it became necessary to establish securo-feminists there too. As President Bush put it, Iraqi women had to have rights because "the security of our own citizens depends on it." The continuing American march to "advance of freedom in the Greater Middle East," Bush claimed, has "given new rights and new hopes to Iraqi women" who would "play an essential part in rebuilding the nation." [12] Upholding "women's dignity" was, in this view, directly linked to fighting terrorism since "men and women with dignity do not strap bombs to their bodies and kill innocent people." American values respected women's right to equality, and so the imposition of American values was crucial to getting people in these lesser states to learn to respect women's rights. There was, in the grammar of the War on Terror, only one way to get to gender parity, and it was in the establishment of American-style liberal democratic institutions.

Securo-feminism, thus, bound white American feminism to the neoimperial and neoliberal project of nation-building around the world—one that Harvard professor and historian Niall Ferguson had articulated in his theory of "Anglobalization," proposing that young Americans should be taught to go overseas and transform other nations in their own image much as Britain had done. Caught in its fevers, American feminists did not question loudly enough the wisdom of exporting feminism through bombs and drones. Trickle-down feminism, everyone assumed, would miraculously fast-forward the realization of a gender-equal, free-market world created in the self-image of America.

In 2012, securo-feminism gained even more clout by

becoming *the* basis upon which the United States would engage with other women around the world. In the words of Jane Mosbacher Morris, who drafted the first "U.S. Women and Counter-terrorism" strategy and the U.S. Counter-terrorism Department's plan on Women, Peace, and Security, "We really started to solidify what the different ways are in which you can engage women on the issues of terrorism and counter-terrorism and what as a department we can be doing to get women to engage."[13] The new plan wanted women in countries involved in the War on Terror to engage in "counter-messaging and other examples of the fight against terror." A 2016 report by the U.S. Institute for Peace (USIP) declared, "Women's rights and place in society are central to the narratives of violent extremist groups, and these narratives are the terrain on which women in Afghanistan fight to establish their rights." The argument being that since terror groups wanted to limit women's rights, women should be enlisted in fighting them. Feminism thus was fighting terrorism. Notably this meant only that "Countering Violent Extremism (CVE) and Preventing Violent Extremism (PVE) needs to include women as target groups."[14] Notably, there was no mention of investing in Afghan women's political participation, perhaps because if Afghan women had political freedom they would prioritize ending the American occupation over anything else. Instead, the goal was to train Afghan women to be puppets that would parrot whatever their American CVE or PVE instructors taught them.

In the paradigm set out by this strategy, if women were unwilling to accept the American assumption that most of their young men were terrorists, and to collaborate with American forces in interrogating, imprisoning, or killing them, then it must be assumed they were also against women's empowerment. In this way, supporting America's foreign-policy interests had become synonymous with feminism.

One particularly distressing example of the high cost to feminist progress exacted by the war is what happened in Pakistan after the capture of Osama bin Laden in Abbottabad, Pakistan, in 2011. In the run-up to his capture, the CIA and the U.S. military allegedly worked with the charity Save the Children in hiring Dr. Shakil Afridi, a Pakistani physician, to run a fake Hepatitis B vaccination program as a front for their surveillance operations.[15] Per CIA instructions, Dr. Afridi and a female healthcare worker visited the bin Laden compound under the guise of administering vaccinations and managed to gain access, although they did not see bin Laden. In 2012, all foreign Save the Children staff were expelled from Pakistan, and in 2015, the entire organization there was required to shut its doors, despite having denied (and continuing to deny) that it was involved in this effort.

The CIA managed to get their guy, but when the Pakistanis, irate at not having been told about the raid, expelled U.S. military trainers from Islamabad, they were immediately threatened with a cut of the $800 million aid package that the U.S. had promised, thus exposing yet again the coercive power that aid wields. The loss of aid money was not, however, the worst impact of the tragedy. As the British medical journal *The Lancet* reported, the unintended victims of the tragedy were the millions of Pakistani children whose parents now refused to have them vaccinated amidst rising rates of polio, a disease that vaccination had essentially extinguished in Western countries by the mid-twentieth century.[16] In their view, if the CIA could hire a doctor to run a fake vaccine program, then the whole premise of vaccinations became untrustworthy. Within a few years of the raid, Pakistan had 60 percent of all the world's confirmed polio cases.[17]

Then there was the targeting of Pakistan's Lady Health Worker Program. Developed in 1994, the program trains Pakistani women in basic healthcare.[18] In a country that is struggling to give its women a voice, the program represents a bold woman-centered step forward that has actually increased the availability of healthcare for millions of Pakistani women who would otherwise have none. The health workers go from house to house, covering both remote rural areas and overpopulated urban ones (both constituencies in desperate need of better healthcare provision), disbursing basic preventive and clinical care, including prenatal and postnatal support and, of course, vaccinations.

When vaccinations became suspect, so too did these health workers; their vans and convoys were attacked by terrorist groups like the Tehreek-e-Taliban Pakistan, which was running its own antivaccination/intimidation campaign. On November 26, 2014, four vaccinators were gunned down in Baluchistan, Pakistan. Earlier that same year a health worker named Salma Farooqi was kidnapped, tortured, and murdered in the Pakistani city of Peshawar.[19] The killings have continued, the latest occurring in April 2019, when women were shot at and one killed, finally leading to the suspension of Pakistan's anti-polio vaccination drive.[20]

The example illustrates how white feminists' uncritical acceptance of the goals and strategies of the War on Terror fails woefully to account for the harm to feminist initiatives like the Pakistan Lady Health Worker Program. Once again, Brown women and Brown children were left facing the costs and consequences of the political actions of white women and their governments. The Save the Children episode was cleverly omitted from Zero Dark Thirty, as were most other accounts of the raid, conveniently side-stepping any discourse on the decision to endanger healthcare provision to millions of Brown women and children. The question that it poses is whether it is the lady health workers of Pakistan, meeting their community's needs even under the threat of their own lives, or the torture-happy women of the CIA, who are the real feminist heroines of the bin Laden story.

———

It is not just the United States that is guilty of doublespeak on feminism. In 2014, Sweden, led by their newly installed center-left foreign minister, Margot Wallström, announced that it was going to have a "feminist" foreign policy. The text of the resolution read: "Equality between women and men is a fundamental aim of Swedish foreign policy. Ensuring that women and girls can enjoy their fundamental human rights is both an obligation within the framework of our international commitments, and a prerequisite for reaching Sweden's broader foreign policy goals on peace, and security and sustainable development."[21]

The year after the policy was launched, Wallström addressed a parliamentary committee, saying that given the country's new feminist foreign policy, the Swedes would not export arms to countries that did not meet its democracy criterion. The main country at issue was Saudi Arabia, whose use of arms and intimidation to harass Saudi women's rights activists was well known. However, in 2017 a civil society group discovered that Sweden's arms-export relationship with Saudi Arabia was never ceased and arms exports have continued. In September 2019, after a bombing by Saudi aircraft that killed around 100 people, Wallström said that she would "speak to as many people as possible." Listening, however, is unlikely to help a situation in which, according to a Swedish television report, Saudi Arabia continues to use Swedish arms to bomb Yemenis, displacing hundreds of thousands and killing at least 10,000. Despite its "feminist" foreign policy, Sweden remains the fifteenth largest arms exporter in the world.[22]

Canada also deserves a special mention in this regard because they are so insistent in casting their interventions and policies as located within the nexus of "feminism." In 2017, Canadian foreign minister Chrystia Freeland announced that the country was spearheading a "feminist international assistance policy" that had been developed after consultations with 15,000 people in sixty countries. Under the umbrella of the new policy, Canada would be spending billions of Canadian dollars toward "advancing gender equality" and "empowering women and girls." The percentage of the total International Assistance Budget devoted to development projects geared toward this goal was to be increased from 1–2 percent to about 90 percent.

Despite feminist "good intentions," however, Canada's International Assistance Budget had already been committed by the previous government of Prime Minister Harper until 2020, leaving no funds to support Freeland's claims.[23] Additionally, experts such as scholar Jessica Cadesky noted that the policy conflated "gender equality" with "women's empowerment," depoliticizing or over-politicizing gender to fit the government's policy proposals. At the same time, the country refused demands by the Canadian Labour Organization and other rights groups such as Amnesty International Canada to implement measures that would allow them to report and track arms sales to foreign countries, including the United States.[24] In June 2020, Canada doubled its arms sales to Saudi Arabia, despite having criticized the country for its abysmal human-rights record and having placed a moratorium on further arms exports.[25] A September 2020 report by the United Nations declared that Canada was "fueling war" in Yemen; the United States, the United Kingdom, and France were also mentioned in the report as enablers.

So even while it has not spent or allocated new funds toward realizing the feminist foreign assistance policy and is continuing to sell arms to countries such as the United States and Saudi Arabia, Canada is enjoying the inherent virtue signaling that comes from adopting something "feminist."[26] The scenario deserves the attention of feminists because it (yet again!) reveals how the branding of feminism is directed largely toward white women, in this case Canadian white women, who want to feel good about their country and gloss over all the many unfeminist acts in which Canada is complicit.

It is not only CIA agents and development bureaucrats and nation-states that have co-opted the language of feminism; it is also journalists. If the former create and manage the conditions of war, the latter shapes its narrative. The image of the War on Terror as a feminist war to deliver rights to women around the world could not have been established without State Department spokeswomen, CIA operatives, and other women directly associated with the war project. But American journalists, *female* journalists in particular, created a narrative for the War on Terror that reaffirmed it as one fought by a feminist America against antifeminist, primitive, patriarchal, and premodern countries that were too apathetic or too weak or too traitorous to fight terror in their homelands themselves.

In one such 2015 article from the *New York Times*, journalist Alissa Rubin calls out "women's shelters as the most provocative legacy of the Western presence in Afghanistan."[27] It is an alarming claim, given that by the time the article was written, the most provocative legacy might have been the graves of 11,000 Afghans killed in the war just that year, a record high adding to the total of hundreds of thousands of casualties.[28] The very idea of helping women or establishing shelters, Rubin tells *Times* readers, was "a revolutionary idea in Afghanistan—every bit as alien as Western democracy and far more transgressive." While it is undoubted that women taking refuge at government-run shelters was not a recourse that existed before the arrival of the Americans, it is also true that violence against women in general was increased by the American presence, and the breakdown of family and tribal support structures.

A scene from *Whiskey Tango Foxtrot*, a movie starring

Tina Fey and based on *Chicago Tribune* journalist Kim Barker's memoir *The Taliban Shuffle*, is representative of this condescending dynamic. In the book, Barker describes her interaction with an Afghan woman who befriends her at a wedding as feeling like "a first date with a mime." Afghan women are mimics trying to mime the liberation modeled by white women journalists who have come to write the stories about them and teach them about feminism.

Heroines of American journalism writing in publications like the *New York Times* and the *Washington Post* and reporting for major television networks have all played a similar role of legitimizing America's neoimperial project in Afghanistan and Iraq and the Middle East at large, promoting a narrative that violent military incursions are designed to liberate women and deliver better societies. Thus they also underscore their own superior status as white feminists, with their values of rebellion (over resilience), risk (over caution), and speed (over endurance) as the ultimate feminist values. Afghan women emerge as no more than prototypes whose wishes always align with what white feminists think they should want, rather than as people with independent political positions and perspectives.

Some of the tactics deployed by white women in particular in reporting on the Middle East and on Muslim women are a savage allegory of the self-serving nature of white feminism. Many offered a "friendship," or rather the construction of a framework of "sisterhood," to gain access into the lives of the women they wished to report on. Åsne Seierstad, for example, author of the bestselling *The Bookseller of Kabul*, freely admits that she capitalized on the Afghan cultural formality of offering hospitality and moved into a family's house to get material for her book, and that she "never mastered Dari,"[29] but it seems she felt completely entitled to represent the innermost thoughts of the women of the family who spoke only that language. The resulting stories, for which the writers are paid (but the subjects/tellers are not), betray their subjects' confidence or, at best, appear startlingly insensitive to their subjects' feelings. Worse, having no enduring relationship to the community, these white writers generally disappear from the lives of their subjects the second the stories are filed, apparently with no regard to the emotional, political, and practical consequences of their exposures and betrayals. Such consequences are exemplified by a lawsuit that the bookseller's second wife brought against Seierstad for defamation and negligent journalistic practices. Among other things, the suit alleged that Seirstand's disclosures of certain sexual behaviors had forced some of the women to emigrate to avoid the censure or worse that they would have suffered as a result of those disclosures if they had stayed in Afghanistan. Ultimately, a Norwegian appeals court reversed a lower-court judgment against Seierstad, but the case dragged on for more than a decade.

The intimate space in Middle Eastern and Afghan households have proven maddening ciphers for Western journalists seeking to decode the mysterious lives of Muslim terrorists and their women. The consequence of this segregated arrangement has meant that male journalists reporting from Muslim countries often have access to only half the world and hence half the story. Some, like the pho-

tographer who accompanied *Times* journalist Rod Nordland in Afghanistan, have pretended to not understand that
men are not permitted to enter certain spaces, barging into
women's quarters to take pictures—in this case, of a young
woman, the subject of a story Nordland was reporting on
honor killings, who had retreated to the women's quarters
of the house expressly to avoid his invasive attentions.[30]

The segregation of female space has in turn created
opportunity for Western female journalists looking for
ways to succeed in the often sexist, male-dominated field
of war correspondence. Like the securo-feminists of the
world who want to establish their equality in inflicting
torture on Brown men, white women journalists have
been eager to establish their equality in war journalism by
reporting on the inner lives and sad situations of Muslim
women. Their priority is not feminist solidarity but gender
parity with white men in professional advancement.

Some white female journalists have pointed to this in
their public statements: famed anchor Katie Couric called
the Gulf War a proving ground that made the female journalist a "ten," and the steady supply of wars since have
produced many more tens.[31] Christiane Amanpour of
CNN, Lara Logan of CBS, award-winning photojournalist
Lynsey Addario, and many lesser-known reporters have
descended into the women's spaces of Iraq and Afghanistan, Pakistan and Saudi Arabia, Yemen and Somalia. A
trove of journalistic exposition, much of it highlighting
the secret, underground, hidden nature of these spaces,
has followed, captured in photographs, front-page stories,
and bestselling books that have burnished the profiles and
shored up the finances of these white feminist heroines.

In 2015, for example, Lynsey Addario's memoir, *It's What I Do: A Photographer's Life of Love and War*, became a widely feted bestseller, optioned for film. In it, Addario describes how she chose her job with the *New York Times* to prove herself as a woman in the male-dominated realm of war photography. The success of her series on women in Afghanistan in the wake of 9/11, "Women of Jihad," led to a MacArthur Foundation "genius" grant in 2009. Addario has come to specialize in intimate images of foreign, largely Black and Brown women published in top Western magazines. One particular contribution, featured on the cover of *Time* in 2016, shows a nearly naked Sudanese teenager, pregnant with her rapist's child—an image that no magazine would feature of an American girl. Discussing her 2018 photo book, *Of Love & War*, Addario's own bravery at going out into a war zone is front and center, while the heroism of the civilians actually *enduring* war, imposed by the United States and its allies, never comes up.[32] Addario describes how her access to women's spaces and even her own experience of motherhood helped her reporting, but never acknowledges or questions the opportunism of how she has deployed this "sisterhood," or how whiteness and Americanness played crucial roles in her work, or the power she holds over what part of Afghan women's lives she makes "visible" to the white and Western world.

For many white feminist writers, going "behind the veil" of their benighted sisters? has been a reliable path to success. Former *Chicago Tribune* journalist Kim Barker's memoir, *The Taliban Shuffle: Strange Days in Afghanistan and Pakistan*, was turned into a movie featuring comedienne Tina Fey. Katherine Zoepf, who reported from Egypt and Syria for the *New York Times*, released her own book, *Excellent Daughters: The Secret Lives of Young Women Who Are Transforming the Arab World*. In 2019, Dionne Searcey, the West Africa correspondent for the *Times*, released her memoir, *In Pursuit of Disobedient Women*, the book's very title alluding to the fact that disobedient women (read: women who behave as white feminists think they should) are very hard to find in that region. This list goes on.

It is a convenient coming-together, the gendered divisions of the Muslim world with the individualistic feminist goals of the West, in a time of constant war. Through the tempering medium of a white woman who functions as a moral legitimization chamber, issues of torture and subjugation are transformed into little celebrations of white women's bravery rather than exposures of American cruelty. Americans looking at Addario's photos or Searcey's reporting for the *Times* about Boko Haram will not consider the real impact of the War on Terror, or of America's role in it, simply the "courage" of white women who, like Gertrude Bell a hundred years earlier, have gone riding into the field, realizing their potential as men's equals through the enduring benefits of white privilege revived by American dominance.

There is an assumption in this kind of reporting that bringing the stories to light is somehow beneficial for the women themselves. In one interview, Lynsey Addario says that her photography of Afghan women was an attempt to reveal to readers "who these women really were—if they could see them in their homes, with their children . . . it might offer a more complete picture."[33] In the same way that the purported goal of feminist rescue legitimizes the violence of war, so the claim to be helping their subjects gives white feminist journalists moral carte blanche to use lies and subterfuge freely. When Addario wanted to photograph a secret girls' school under the Taliban, she used a camera "concealed in [her] bag."[34] When an Afghan man (Addario seems to organize her reporting primarily through them) objected to her photographing "his" women, his protestations could be discarded because of their repugnant chauvinism by our highly principled feminist reporter, who unfortunately forgets to tell us in her book how or whether she obtained consent from the women themselves. Addario may have been more careful about getting consent (despite not knowing the language) in other cases, but in this incident, it is unclear if she did so, and her failure to address this in her book suggests that it was not consent, but the photos that were important. There is no discussion of the damage that would be done if the secret school is exposed through her photography. (Of course, it is not only white women who have been accused of this mistake. Steven McCurry, the photographer who took National Geographic's iconic 1985 photograph of the "Afghan girl," recently has been accused of failing to get the girl's consent, a charge he denies.)[35]

When subterfuge is not necessary or not possible, white feminist reporting relies instead on the sort of camaraderie that can elicit details. Katherine Zoepf's prologue in Excellent Daughters finds her ensconced with a group of female Saudi teenagers, one of whom is about to get married. Everyone shares confidences (for example, the bride hopes for a Disney-themed wedding). Zoepf calls on her upbringing as a Jehovah's Witness to assume the task of revealing to us the secrets of these young Saudi women she has befriended. Through Zoepf's words, one feels invited into the fold, escorted into that mysterious world where Muslim women share secrets away from the gaze of men, and usually also the Western reader.

Implying puerility in girls more at ease discussing Disney than their future husbands, or irredeemable backwardness in those who find controversial the issue of talking to a man before being married—Zoepf makes her condescending judgments available only to her readers and not to her Saudi "friends." In other journalistic forays, she focuses on a secret society in Syria, then turns her attention to boy-crazy husband-hunters in liberal Lebanon, relying on the sex-and-the-Orient mix (the chapter is titled "The Most Promiscuous Virgins in the World") that reliably entertains Western readers. Despite knowing this, Zoepf expresses surprise that some of her subjects ask her why she's more interested in these sorts of salacious stories than in "serious Lebanese girls," the ones fighting for better education, harassment-free workplaces, and more equal relationships. To everyone else, the reason should be clear: Zoepf might or might not be trying to elevate and explicate the struggles of other women—or to challenge American ideas about Muslim women—in service of constructing mutual feminist understanding, but what she is actually doing is creating white feminist clickbait.

The lack of accountability in depicting her subjects comes to a head in *Excellent Daughters* when Zoepf discusses the reaction some of her interview subjects have had to some of her stories. In Syria, she interviews Enas, the eighteen-year-old daughter of a woman who runs an

all-female madrassa. Following the story's publication in
the *New York Times*—which "included comments by Enas
and her best friend Fatima, as well as a large photo of
Enas kneeling on a carpet at the girls' madrassa where she
taught"—Zoepf received a distressed phone call from her
teen subject, whose exposure in the newspaper could mean
a "frightening visit to the madrassa from the mukhabarat,
the infamous secret police," and subsequent surveillance
and harassment.[36] There is no helping going on here, with
the lives of women like Enas laid on the line for the careers
of women like Zoepf.

This is the predictable outcome when intimate access
becomes the story and building meaningful sisterhood
is sublimated to personal ambition. Apart from anything
else, it is essential to remember that the purported inti-
macy that these journalists perform should not be mis-
taken for expertise. Addario can speak neither Dari nor
Pashto and by her own admission does not know "much
about Afghanistan aside from *Times* articles" she has read
while on the elliptical.[37] Zoepf has studied Arabic, but the
extent of her proficiency is unclear.

———

The dueling feminisms at work in the uneasy journalist-
as-feminist paradigm mirror the tension between the collective versus individual that are threaded through the
history of women's empowerment. The feminism of sisterhood alleges a universal female affinity bound by the fight
against patriarchy; it is by appealing to this idea that Western female journalists gain access to the intimate spaces of
women of color. It is easy to tell Afghan or Nigerian women

how you, too, are a mother, or you, too, have felt frightened walking down the street alone at night, manufacturing the emotional bonds that forge trust. Ultimately, however, it is the feminism of a ruthless individualism that motivates the behavior of too many white women journalists.

Whether it's serving in the ranks of the CIA and hunting Osama bin Laden, or the "soft" warfare of reporting stories such that they by and large support a neo-imperial, U.S.-centered worldview, white feminists have been front and center in the War on Terror. Carrying forward the racial hierarchies and self-interested exploitation of the colonial era, white feminists have identified progress not as renouncing wars and empire but as competing with white men at the tasks of neo-imperialism.

White feminists in the colonial era were all about spreading their civilized ways, but neo-colonial white feminists want to illustrate their courage and compassion—often while providing moral subsidy for cruelties inflicted in feminism's name. Times may have changed, but the commitment of whiteness to extracting value wherever it can—and dominating the narrative to frame this extraction as benevolence—persists.

—

CHAPTER FIVE

Sexual Liberation Is Women's Empowerment

I first learned about sex-positive feminism in a graduate seminar at a large Midwestern university. Every
Tuesday and Thursday, the long, bare classroom
in the basement of one of the care-worn Liberal Arts
buildings on campus would fill with students eager to
talk about their hook-ups, their predilection for one or
another kind of erotica, and their general affirmation
of the transformative capacities of the sexual act. For
those who weren't there, sex-positive feminism stands
for the precept that women are not free until and unless
they are sexually free. In the competitiveness that graduate seminars breed, my classmates rambled on about
threesomes, triumphant and unceremonious dumpings
of emotionally attached lovers (who has time for attach-
ment?), and in general lots and lots of sex. Every class
unfolded almost as a sort of performance, where sexual identity was what defined each and every student.

Nobody wanted to be "not liberated," and so everyone shared, or rather overshared, compulsively.

Our smug white professor, nose-pierced and wild-haired and duly sporting the scarves and baubles of the well traveled, encouraged it all as a grand doyenne of ceremonies. The question of how and when sexual liberation had become not simply the centerpiece but the entire sum of liberation for a graduate seminar on feminist theory never came up, nor did any discussion of sexual identity and radical politics. The year was 2006.

I was disappointed, but I said nothing. I agreed with sexual liberation as an essential portion of liberation in general; I just wasn't convinced that it was the whole. I was in search of a politics that did more, that used the domination of cisgender over all genders to poke at the similarly oppressive hegemony of whiteness, that discussed who was automatically included under the umbrella of feminism and who was left out. By comparison, this seminar's obsession with sexual activity as the start and end of feminism seemed so limited and immature.

I wasn't older than my fellow students, but I was divorced and a single mother; I spent a lot of my time juggling money and precarious childcare and a constantly pulled and stretched budget; I didn't have much energy to chase the next sexual adventure. Around the same time that I took the seminar, I had just returned from Pakistan, still bruised at having to explain my life choices to a family that had never before seen a divorce. In Pakistan I had worried about somehow losing custody of my daughter, because children were seen as part of the father's family;

in American courts I had had to explain my fitness as a
mother, because I worked and went to school all day and
had less than a strong support system. I had to make the
case that being poor and an immigrant did not make me
a bad mother.

The world I lived in beyond my classes at the university was not one most of my fellow students knew; it was a
world of responsibility, precarity, and survival. And I felt
this difference from my classmates acutely. My brown skin
and my longish tunics sent from Karachi were evidence
enough in themselves, I felt—an indictment of the fact that
I came from a less sexually liberated place and that I was
much less adept at the performance of sexual liberation.
Many of those who had known me growing up in Pakistan
would have laughed if they heard how insecure I felt about
that supposed sexlessness. I had been (and was) the rebel-
in-chief of my class at our school. I was eager to do everything and anything that was not allowed—sneak lipstick,
call random boys on the phone, flirt with anyone who
caught my eye, raise up my trousers to show an ankle, and
generally break every rule that I could. If there was something I was told I absolutely had to do, I just did not want
to do it. Even in the United States, I was one of a handful
of single mothers in my cohort, insistent on graduating
despite the admonishment of white course-load advisers
who had told me that "law school was no place for mothers, especially not single mothers."

But in this graduate seminar, part of the PhD portion
of the JD/PhD degrees I was pursuing, I felt defensive for
other reasons. Being Muslim and female was an identity
that in the view of most liberal academics, and certainly

students, rhymed effortlessly with sexual repression. Few of my classmates had much idea of what life was like in other cultures. So often and in so many other classes I had heard both students and professors invoke the hapless women imprisoned by Islam (or, as my professors and classmates would incorrectly describe them, "Islamic women") as an offhand way to highlight the relative good fortune of the Western feminist.

To make clear I was not one of these oppressed and sexually subjugated women of the Muslim world, I had to *perform* my sexuality. I have seen so many other Brown women do the same since: showing off their love of porn and lewd jokes, talking about what bawdy thing they enjoyed with a husband or boyfriend, anything to underscore that they were sexually liberated and hence empowered. It wasn't about whether they genuinely liked or enjoyed what they talked about—they may well have done, and good for them—but rather that they had to present it in order to be seen as equal to white women. I had no problem at all with people having rich and varied and fulfilling sex lives, or even talking about them. My problem was specifically with the expectation of talking about them as some kind of passport to feminist legitimacy.

There is now a term for this sort of pressure: compulsory sexuality. In her work, scholar Kristina Gupta defines this as evolving from radical feminist Adrienne Rich's definition of "compulsory heterosexuality," which in turn stands for "a system of norms and practices that force women into participating in heterosexuality."[1] Gupta and others identified both sexually repressive societies that denied women sexual liberation and choice, and supposedly sexually liberated societies like the United States that expect women to perform their sexual identity, as manifesting compulsory sexuality. In both cases, "compulsory sexuality" was a means of disciplining others, or as "a vector of regulation." The idea of "asexuality" as an identity has in fact evolved in part to underscore the pressure felt by those who do not wish to ascribe to a commodified sexualized identity.

"Sexusociety" is a similar concept devised by gender scholar Ela Przybylo to describe a compulsorily sexual world. Since it is hard to consider what we are immersed in all the time, Przybylo uses the idea of asexuality, the far opposite of compulsory sexuality, to explain her work. When we consider the world from an asexual lens rather than from the position of any particular sexual identity, we can better apprehend how heterosexuality and, to a far lesser extent, LGBTQI identities have been co-opted as the basis of markets of goods that must be consumed. Consumption of particular products becomes the basis of being considered sexual or sexy. Everybody knows that sex, particularly heteronormative sex, sells, but Przybylo further argues that sex is being used to hide the extent to which capitalism has infiltrated our consideration of our own identity, with heteronormative identity being the most co-opted and LGBTQI identities less so. Asexuality, then, functions not simply as a sexual identity in itself but also as a concept in which the intersection of capitalism and sexual identity politics is revealed. We consume and therefore we are sexual; our sexual identity is thus predicated on capitalist consumption.

Back in graduate school in 2006, I did not have access

to this sort of discussion or understanding to explain my sense of being cornered, forced to express myself in a certain way. I vehemently supported sexual liberation and sexual expression, but I did not understand why this had to be the most important or even the most visible thing about me. The burden of having to prove myself as non–sexually repressed—and thereby earning the label "feminist," worthy of respect and a voice in the room—sat wooden and unrelenting on my shoulders all semester long. Even if I had been able to explain how asexuality helps underscore the lost anti-capitalist potential of a heterosexuality immersed in consumerism, I would have been too afraid to bring it up. *Poor her*, my colleagues might think, *all the repression of her culture has left her an asexual*. In this equation where sexual empowerment equaled all empowerment, there was no room to consider the weight of compulsory sexuality.

No texts by Muslim feminists were assigned reading for the course, no *Women and Gender in Islam* by Leila Ahmed, and no *Qur'an and Woman* by Amina Wadud—texts that would have highlighted how feminism within Islam confronted patriarchy. We spent no more than one hour of class discussion time on it. No class or seminar can cover everything. But this class's lack of inclusion of any save the most Eurocentric perspectives meant that it offered no analytical means of questioning sex-positive feminism. The consensus among my classmates was not even made visible as such—as the hegemony of a single perspective over other alternatives—because our professors didn't consider those alternate perspectives legitimate entries to the canon of feminist theory and literature. The voices in the seminar and in the texts we read were by and large white and mostly privileged, and the reading list indicated to me that it was those voices that mattered.

The exclusion of Muslim feminists in particular from the narrative of feminist thought has been the status quo in the West forever, countered only by sudden spurts of attention to "other" feminists when news events focus on them.

When Gloria Steinem's memoir, *My Life on the Road*, was published in 2015, Steinem named twenty-eight women and three men in her list of "best contemporary feminist writers."[2] The list fails to mention a single Muslim feminist who did not share Steinem's support for the invasion of Afghanistan.[3] I shouldn't have been too surprised— Steinem was a liberal feminist who once worked for the CIA, and continued to serve on the board of organizations for women soldiers and to speak at events where she was billed as a "leading advocate for women in the military."[4]

The Muslim women whom the Western press loves most are the ones who visibly refuse to critique the West, focusing only on what is wrong with Islam/Muslims/Muslim societies, thus validating the colonial thesis that all reform comes from the West. Recent literature on countering violent extremism initiatives supports this, bringing Orientalist mystery and even a sinister eroticism into the plot that centers on Muslim women themselves being sustainers and supporters of the terror agendas of various groups.[5]

It is not simply the right that wants to include Muslim women under the umbrella of guilt in which all Muslim men are automatically implicated as terrorists or potential terrorists. Perhaps especially among self-declared feminists, there is a curious substitution that takes place around Muslim women's sexuality and the monstrous figure of the Muslim terrorist, as I discovered when I wrote an article called "Women and Islamic Militancy" for the Winter 2015 issue of the traditionally left-wing *Dissent* magazine.[6] The central theme of my piece highlighted how some Muslim militant organizations used "empowerment-like" rhetoric to attract women. I noted how the exclusion of Muslim women from the central narrative of Western feminism contributed to the power of this appeal. The article was considered so problematic by the editors of *Dissent* that it was published with a "response" from a "real" feminist, who unsuccessfully tried to take down my arguments by listing the Islamic State's sins against women (as if I had missed them all); speculating about whether sixteen-year-old Islamic State recruits are mature enough to make political decisions; and providing a history of the conservative opposition to women's movements in general. Not long after publication, Michael Walzer, one of *Dissent*'s editors in chief, professor of political philosophy at Princeton, gave an interview in which he accused me of being "fascinated and even excited" by the idea of a Muslim "woman warrior" and terrorist killing.[7]

Here, then, was liberal Islamophobia, painting me as less than rational, ruled by emotions and sinister obsessions rather than intellectual interest and critical questioning. With that one comment I was banished from the realm of rational discussion, as too female, too Muslim, too unqualified to be spoken to directly, only to be derided in print and subject to insinuations. Just as racism and misogyny mixed in the trial and prosecution of Tituba, an enslaved woman accused of witchcraft in 1600s Salem,

Massachusetts, so too did Orientalism, racism, and misogyny blend in Walzer's characterization of my "fascinations."

In my interpretation, Walzer's suggestion that I was somehow titillated by terror deployed the Orientalist notion that, being Muslim, I was too repressed to find sexual pleasure through sex itself and was instead deriving erotic satisfaction from the fantasy of terrorist killing.

———

Sexual liberation and feminism were not always conflated. The Sexual Revolution of the 1960s onward saw recognition and popularization of the idea that women, like men, had sexual needs and desires and should have the freedom to pursue them. The women's liberation movement, initiated much earlier, had broader goals, such as gender equality, access to job opportunities, and freedom from violence and harassment at the workplace and at home. The two became conflated in the 1970s and '80s as both were colonized by capitalism. The emergence of women as economic actors beyond the household, their wallets full of money they earned themselves, created a new category of consumer. Some proponents of women's lib wanted to be seen as sexy, which meant that advertisers could lure them with images of the sexually liberated woman wearing a certain kind of lingerie, buying makeup and fashion items, smoking a certain kind of cigarette, and drinking a certain kind of alcohol. A 1972 print ad for Bulova watches shows male and female arms with matching his and hers watches and the slogan "Equal Pay, Equal Time"; a Virginia Slims commercial shows a woman in tight pants bending down and the slogan "They're slim-

mer than the thick cigarettes men smoke." Newport cigarettes developed an entire campaign around the sexually
liberated and economically empowered woman's search
for gratification: "Alive with Pleasure."[8]

The energy and attention of the ordinary woman who,
a few years earlier, might have marched for equal pay was
now co-opted and directed toward hanging out at newly
built malls, buying this or that social signifier. Sex is good
marketing material, and a sexy feminism could be directed
toward the purchase of allegedly empowering products.
This sexy feminism was less concerned with the collective
of "all" women or with feminist solidarity than it was with
the individual, her quest for pleasure and her desire to get
ahead. It was this process of corporate colonization that cut
down the political possibilities of the feminist movement.
Political transformation was out; increasing the individual
woman's buying power, making her a better specimen of
Homo economicus, was in.

With the infamous decade of "free love" just drawn to a
close, and the Sexual Revolution it kickstarted long under
way, the central thesis of Kate Millett's *Sexual Politics*—
that the sexual act is imbued with the power differentials
that operate in a patriarchal society—had particular relevance. Toward this end, Millett took apart the work of
then-"progressive" writers Henry Miller, D. H. Lawrence,
and Norman Mailer. What passed for risqué and erotic,
she asserted, was really just normalizing ways of demean-
ing, degrading, and subjugating women. Sexual liberation,
Millett wrote, could not be the sum total of women's liberation, because sex could also be a venue for the perpetuation of patriarchy. Feminism could not leave this realm

unaddressed if it wanted to bring about equality and harness the real power of the Sexual Revolution. Empowerment for women, Millett argued, required radical political action, with women's energy targeted toward dismantling the structures of capitalism that were similarly dominated by men. For Millett, it was the unraveling of systems of power that would ultimately lead to equality for women. If the Sexual Revolution was recognizing women's sexual needs, *Sexual Politics* was exposing how women had been used as objects to satisfy male needs. If the Sexual Revolution wanted women to own their sexuality, Millett wanted the new feminist consciousness to provoke scrutiny of gender relations and the subsequent development of a radical politics that would tear down misogynistic systems of power and control.

At the time, it appeared that this analysis and critical estimation of the power differentials within sex (heterosexual and otherwise) would be the next step in the women's movement. When Millett's book was published in 1979, it was a bestseller, and she was feted as a darling of the feminist movement. She was even featured on the cover of *Time*, her critical analysis of sex deemed prescient during a tumultuous era.

Neither her renown nor the centrality of her thesis would endure. Perhaps critiquing the heterosexual act as being linked to oppression and feminism's project as inherently tied to dismantling the excesses of capitalism was asking for too much change too fast. Better to applaud women who embraced sex as enactors of sexual and feminist liberation, to call them empowered and encourage the idea that the consumption of certain goods, Virginia Slims cigarettes or Maybelline lipstick, were an exercise of feminist power. In the end, it was the sexy corporate feminism connecting liberation with conspicuous consumption that won the day. By the 1990s no one was reading *Sexual Politics* and no academic institution was willing to give Millett a permanent teaching position. In a sense, her fate represented the fate of radical politics as a once-upon-a-time cornerstone of feminist organizing and action.

The first epoch of white feminism, the "first wave," represented struggles around suffrage.[9] The second wave, to which Millett belonged, saw the simultaneous emergence of radical antiestablishment politics and the opening up of a huge number of economic opportunities. In this sense, the second wave saw two competing and interconnected feminisms, the radical feminist committed to remaking social and political structures and the working girl who was eager to make the most of newly emerging opportunities. By the time the third wave came along in the 1990s, radical politics was nowhere to be found. As Gen-Xers took the helm to continue the work begun by the second wave, it was evident which of the two strands, radical versus working girl, had won.

The woman who laid the foundation for a corporate-friendly working-girl feminism was Helen Gurley Brown. Seven years before Kate Millett wrote *Sexual Politics*, Brown published her bestseller *Sex and the Single Girl*. In that book, Brown, a scrappy transplant from Arkansas, told young women to become financially independent and have sexual relationships before they got married. Allegedly, the book was conceived when Brown's then-husband told her that she should consider writing a book detailing how a young single woman goes about having an affair. *Sex and the Single Girl*, which sold millions of copies, was followed up by *Sex and the Office*, in which Brown gives women a how-to on using their femininity and sexuality to get ahead at work.

Brown had a platform that allowed her to reach into the homes of middle-class American women, particularly those who were just beginning to join the workforce. As editor of *Cosmopolitan* until 1997, Brown championed a wily feminism centered on a love for sexual adventure (always heteronormative) and the clever use of feminine sexuality to "get ahead" as she herself had done. Brown was one of the first women to present young American women with the idea that they could have it all—"all" meaning love, sex, and money. She poured these ideas into the magazine to create the "Cosmo Girl," whom the *New York Times* described as "self-made, sexual and supremely ambitious."[10] The Cosmo Girl "looked great, wore fabulous clothes and had an unabashedly good time when the clothes came off."

This sort of feminism was marketable. Helen Gurley Brown was a great champion of conspicuous consumption. Cosmo Girl feminism was not predicated on the protests and contestations of the radical feminists of the women's movement. Advertisers filled (and continue to fill) the pages of the magazine, peddling clothes, perfumes, handbags, and all the other things that women, now converted to economic producers and consumers, were supposed to buy, along with endless tips on sexually pleasing men in bed.

Dating, finding, and keeping a man were the main concerns of *Cosmo* editors under Brown, and the magazine's transactional vocabulary was a giveaway as to how women were being encouraged to look at romantic relationships under the rubric of a sort of economics. As Moira Weigel has so astutely pointed out in her book *Labor of Love*, women were encouraged to "shop around" and "not to settle" and play "hard to get."

Cosmo sex had no political or intellectual overtones; it was instead another product, something in which women could engage but that centered first on their making themselves more attractive to men with the help of the magazine's advertisers. And the disingenuous emphasis on sexual freedom tamed a more radical version of feminism to fit capitalist society. Instead of taking on the thorny business of how sex itself replicates patriarchy in complex ways, sex was made into a commodity that could be consumed by both men and women. And if sex was understood as a commodity that women were choosing to consume, then the morally problematic objectification of women could be replaced by the apparently morally neutral objectification of sex. Women *chose* to purchase makeup or high heels or bigger breasts, not to please men but to enhance their own self-esteem and their capacity to enjoy the liberation of sex. At the same time, the focus shifted away from oppressive institutions of the state and law to the woman herself as a consumer. She carried the power of self-definition and self-determination in her wallet.

The problem was that the "choices" women had were largely constructed by market capitalism. Women, now seen as consumers, were repeatedly accosted with questions of whether they wanted this lipstick or that one, this purse or that one. But even as these specific choices were being presented, the actual realm of choices available to women was shrinking. Even as they became more powerful as consumers or even as decision-makers in their professional spheres, they became less powerful in defining the choices that they wanted. Women now could choose among multiple brands of laundry detergent, but deferred or neglected opportunities to organize politically to demand free childcare for all women.

Consumer capitalism beguiled with choices. These choices presented the illusion of power and control in the constant this-or-that, which is the basis of shopping. And the shopper is always an individual woman. She can choose to buy this car or that car, this house or that house, exercising economic power even while women's collective power beyond consumer choice slips away. Capitalism relies on the individual, and therefore it valorizes the individual. It finds politics, with its agitation and collectivism, a threat to its colonization of all human activity for the purpose of profit, and so it demonizes it. In the tug of war between two strands of feminism, the radical feminists, women who had organized collectively and whose demands for equality had been expressed collectively, and the cash-happy Cosmo Girls interested largely in amassing power in the form of economic capital, the latter had won. By the time Helen Gurley Brown retired in 1997, radical feminists had all but disappeared from the feminist firmament.

———

The cult of the individual became the norm, along with its accompanying expression of power through consumer choice and accrual of capital. The focus of feminism had shifted: instead of aspiring to develop consensus and build solidarity based on what was good for all women, women were rewarded and even celebrated for looking out for themselves. The "self-made" woman rose to take her place as companion to the "self-made" man in the Western mythos of success. But while consumer choices increased, large corporations rather than small businesses dominated the making and selling of products that women used, concentrating the actual power generated by this profit in a small number of corporate executives at the helm of enormous multinational companies.[11] And even as the individual was muscled up as agent of purchasing power, her power as an employee of those corporate bosses dwindled. Meanwhile, female-targeted self-help books proliferated, encouraging women to conclude that any sense of dissatisfaction was their own individual problem—one that could be solved, like everything else, by buying something. One written by Gloria Steinem herself was titled *Revolution from Within: A Book of Self-Esteem*. In its pages, Steinem turned away from the politics of organizing women to defining the problem as an inner one of women's self-image.

Sex remained at the heart of this vision of a modern feminist, birthing an easygoing, pop-feminism crystallized in the hit television show *Sex and the City*. In particular, Samantha's infamously voracious sexual appetite was lauded as testament to the equality that the Sexual Revolution had "won" for women. *Sex and the City* was so enduringly popular and considered such a landmark of feminist progress that it has subsequently become a frame through which white, Western feminists measure the relative empowerment of other countries too. As recently as 2018, almost fifteen years after *Sex and the City* finished airing on TV, the *New York Times* reviewed *An African City*, a Ghanian comedy-drama in which five women look for love in Accra. The *Times* delighted in the fact that the show's characters "fit perfectly into Carrie- or Miranda-type boxes" and are "as free and liberal about sex as their American foremothers."[12] Other similarities receive less attention; the article does not mention that the characters' lifestyles are more or less a work of fantasy, economically near-impossible for most viewers. But issues of class do not concern the creators of *Sex and the City* and its successors; as long as characters make sexually provocative statements and model high levels of feminine consumption, who wants to worry about the realities of women's lives? Delusional aspiration to the lives of upper-middle-class white women from one of the most financially unequal cities in the world, whose great achievement is acting out the myth that sexual freedom is the sum total of empowerment and liberation—a hollow feminism based on consumerism with a bit of sexual liberation thrown in as distraction—that's an American product that can be exported internationally.

Beneath the popularity of *Sex and the City* lay the white feminists' belief that they were the ones to discover the idea of women's sexual pleasure and its liberatory potential. In this mythology, women everywhere through all time were sexually repressed until white women discovered female sexual pleasure and set about teaching it to the rest of the world's women. Once the limitations of this individualistic, consumerist version of feminist progress were set aside, the other problem with white feminists' export of sexual liberation is their fervent belief that they are indeed exporting it to parts of the world that have barely heard the word "sex" before white culture arrived to smash the taboo. In 2019, the *New York Times* reviewed a Senegalese show called *Mistress of a Married Man*, which is typified by moments like the one where protagonist Mareme points to her own crotch and remarks, "This is mine. I give it to whoever I want." Making sweeping assumptions about Senegal, the *Times* writer contrasts the revolutionary, norm-challenging model of sexual liberation handed down by Carrie and Samantha with "a culture where women's sexuality is behind a curtain of discretion."[13] But Senegal, a former French colony, was once far more sexually open and permissive than either the United States or Europe; in the nineteenth century, French administrators lamented the permissive "moral education" and the "corrupting influence of local populations."[14]

India, the country that gave us some of the world's most ancient sexual texts, gets no better treatment. "There's plenty of casual sex," enthuses the *New York Times* reviewer of an Indian show, *Four More Shots Please*, while predictably describing the series as India's own *Sex and the City*. But to maintain the implicit hierarchy of the Western "mainstream" and the limited "progress" made by India, the journalist considers it necessary to mention that "conservative viewers have complained that the show has too much sex."[15]

Sex and the City traffics in the myth that sexual liberation was "discovered" by pioneering white women who like high heels and date emotionally unavailable men. The assumption is that as a society evolves it becomes more sexually liberated; white, Western societies, having evolved, are further along in the march of progress than non-Western ones. And yet the very sexual conservatism that is lamented as a sign of backwardness in non-white societies was in fact a gift of colonizing white and Western powers. Just as white Westerners are now eager to liberate women from sexual prudery and repression, they were eager to enforce sexual constraints on the cultures they colonized a mere century and a half earlier.

Before British colonialization, it was normal for people in India to enjoy nonmonogamous relationships. There were Hindu sects in which women had multiple partners, as well as Muslim men who married multiple women for life or even contracted temporary marriages for just a short-lived dalliance. All of these arrangements recognized the limitations of the monogamous marital relationship that was the only form of marriage known to and recognized/enforced by colonizing Europeans. And of course other sexual relationships took place between consenting adults, such as a rich merchant taking on a dancing girl as a mistress or a widowed or unmarried woman of means taking a younger lover. Homosexual and transgender relationships also existed in plain view, something that was quite alarming to British colonists. Some transgender individuals worked inside the women's quarters of wealthy homes and others in some of the pleasure quarters of Indian cities like Lucknow and Delhi, where the Mughal court had once provided reliable clients.

By contrast, in the same period in Britain, monogamous heterosexual relationships conducted within marriage were the only acceptable form of sexual contact.

Unlike India with its many religions, sects, and modes of belief, Britain in the same period was a religious state with its governance closely connected to the Anglican Church; heterosexual monogamy was part of a Christian moral code, not, as some white people unthinkingly assume, a "natural moral code." During their two-hundred-year period of control of India, the British were intent on "civilizing" their domain by enforcing their own social and cultural norms—including those around sex.[16] If the colonial British were to come up with a television show based on their beliefs and norms around sex, it would have been called *Punishing Sex in the City*. Just as modern Westerners caricature all non-Western societies as grotesquely sexually repressed and stunted, so nineteenth-century whites assumed that non-Western societies were too promiscuous.

In both cases, the desire is nothing to do with the true knowledge and understanding of another culture, and it's not even anything to do with sex. It is about domination of the other. In the absence of any real evidence of these imagined dangers, the white colonizers simply changed the rules and set about creating "crimes" with which to indict the local population. Once native women were classified as sexual deviants, their moral inferiority was established in the eyes of the British public, giving the colonial presence the imprimatur of being reformist. Under British colonial rule, the Contagious Diseases Act of 1868 and the Cantonment Act of 1864 were passed to control and criminalize a vast array of Indian women's sexual behaviors by creating spaces of race-based segregation. Some of the clauses of the Cantonment Act required Indian prostitutes who served white British soldiers to live in quarters adjoining the cantonment so that they were separated from the local population and had sex exclusively with white men. The British also created classifications of "prostitution" through legislation whose vagueness and breadth would give them power over the largest number of women. High-caste Hindu polygamy, Brahmin widowhood, orders of female religious mendicants, various forms of public performance and even Muslim marriage practices suddenly fell into the realm of "prostitution" because they did not mimic the heterosexual, monogamous marriages of the white colonists themselves. In the view of one British magistrate, Alexander Abercrombie, Muslim women "were more sexually brazen than their Hindu counterparts with their insatiable sexual appetites and a dangerous promiscuity."[17] And prostitutes existed "as a result of the insatiable sexual nature of Hindoo women who were unable to restrain themselves despite strict Hindu strictures because of their love of excitement."[18]

Mimicking the gender-based double standards of Britain and to ensure the cooperation of native men in the colonial project, heterosexual male sexual behavior was left alone. Meanwhile, the colonial administration subjected its newly created "prostitutes" to forcible genital examinations., making the bodies of a majority of Indian women subject to literal scrutiny by the British colonial administration. Even while the laws against abortion in England at the time were rarely if ever enforced, the crimes of infanticide and feticide were created as legislative categories with criminal consequences in India, where they were vigorously enforced.[19]

Similar legal restrictions, and the associated violations of human rights, were put in place by the British in Hong Kong. Women were assigned different places to live within and outside the cantonment areas based on which men they "served." The women who serviced white European soldiers had to live within the cantonment and had severe restrictions applied to their freedom of movement. They were also subject to forced genital exams. These sorts of ordinances were still being implemented by British colonists as late as 1939, sometimes as punishments for protests. In that year, a group of Herrero women in central Namibia held a "protest" in which they declared that their country was infected with a poison that could only be removed by a healer. The British decided that the poison referenced in the protest was venereal disease and immediately instituted laws that required unmarried Black women to submit to forced genital examinations for the purpose of rooting out venereal disease.

A variety of strictures and laws toward controlling female sexual behavior were enacted all throughout the British Empire under the pretext of "civilizing" the local female population. The reasons, beyond the overt misogyny of it all, was that the British needed the cooperation of males in order to rule; for example, Indian soldiers served in the British Army and quite literally permitted the vast machinery of the empire to function. Limits on what they could do would thus have been a greater problem for the British, perhaps even fomenting more rebellions in the late nineteenth century and onward. The consequence was that the sexual regulation of Indian society by the British

state occurred almost solely through the control and clas-
sification of women.[20]

———

The case of Kally Bewah, a high-caste Hindu woman who
was found dead in a shack near her home in colonial Calcutta, is an example of how even the body of a dead Indian
woman could be used as evidence of her moral depravity
and inadequacy as a mother and a woman. The story is
illustrative of how the bodies of women who may simply
have died during childbirth were made into specimens that
testified to their inherent inadequacies as moral subjects.

The body of Kally Bewah had been found nude and
partially decomposing with bloodied clothes lying
under her head. The coroner of West Bengal, a man
named E. M. Chambers, conducted the autopsy some-
time before December 14, 1885, and then summarized his
findings in a letter to the Jury of Inquest.[21] Chambers con-
jectured that Kally Bewah, being an upper-class Brahmin
widow, must, as a very ordinary matter of course, have
been "unchaste" and engaged in illicit sex, then hidden the
fact that she had sex outside marriage by trying to procure
an abortion. If Kally Bewah was dead, it was because she
more or less deserved to be. Her body was not the basis of
any actual investigation into her cause of death; it was only
proof that Hindu culture made its insatiable women into
baby-killing sexual deviants.

Unsurprisingly, the jury of white colonial officials
agreed with this interpretation, writing, "We are of the
opinion that Kally Bewah was really pregnant and the
inflammation of the womb from the effects of which Kally

died was the result of criminal abortion or miscarriage." They concluded that in doing so Bewah "committed a rash and negligent act for which she should be committed under Section 304 of Indian Penal Code" and for "concealing birth" under a separate code.

Kally Bewah was already dead and obviously could not be committed anywhere, but that was beside the point. At the time the laws against abortion in England were rarely, if ever, enforced, and yet the crimes of infanticide and feticide were vigorously enforced by the British in India, as further illustration of the moral contrast between the local population and the paragons of virtuous white society.[22] The objective of the autopsy was never to collect evidence and find Bewah's killer. It was instead to collect evidence to indict her culture, to garner support for the fantasy that Indian women were sexually promiscuous to the point of criminality and could only be "reformed" through colonial intervention.

Wrapped up with this assumption of self-abortion was the implication that Brown women were inherently deficient mothers, prone to neglecting and even killing their children. This assumption about mothers of color, contrasted with the Victorian archetype of the white matriarch as "the angel in the hearth," persists today. Within the United States, Black mothers have been typecast for decades as "crack mothers." This is simply another criminalizing framework baldly used to prompt assumptions about the moral worth of a racial group. In the modern version of this rhetorical sleight of hand, it also conveniently obscures the economic conditions, created by white people in power, which drive the very cycles of poverty, addiction, and crime that those white people then condemn as intrinsic. Likewise, Latina mothers are characterized as "breeders": having many children but unable to support those children—another symptom of economic suppression by white people that those white people then weaponize as evidence of inferiority. And following exactly the same pattern, Native American mothers are stereotyped as alcoholics, associated in the white imagination with fetal alcohol syndrome beyond all proportion to reality, and with no consideration paid to the white-authored conditions that drive up addiction rates within a financially and culturally dispossessed community.[23]

From colonialism to neo-colonialism, whole populations are dismissed with the image of the failed non-white mother, held up as evidence of moral inferiority and the incontrovertible need for Western altruism. The deep-rooted existence of these assumptions are visibly co-opted by adoption agencies like Adoption Help International, whose website explains that "the easiest way to understand the type of child/children that become available for adoption in Guatemala is to realize the processes of 'abandonment' and 'relinquishment' at work." Abandonment, according to this rubric, is "when a child has been abandoned by his/her biological family, or when parental rights have been terminated by the Guatemalan government due to neglect," and relinquishment is "when a Guatemalan mother relinquishes the child's care to a lawyer because of her inability to give maternal care." The implication of a widespread crisis in Guatemalan motherhood, one prompting a dedicated terminology by its sheer ubiquity, invites white U.S. mothers to step in and rescue those children.[24]

The non-white mother (then and now) is "subalternized," or rendered voiceless, sandwiched between the patriarchal pressures of her own culture and the nobility of the white mother. White women's behavior exists in perfect moderation in contrast to non-white mothers, all either too repressed or too incontinent to be appropriate role models to their own children, who are then available for rescue by acquisitive white women.

———

At the end of my term studying feminist theory in graduate school, I wrote a paper about the efforts to repeal a Pakistani law that criminalizes fornication and adultery (one of the Hudood Ordinances). I argued that reform in Pakistan had to be culturally and religiously relevant. One of the analytical texts I offered as an example was written by a University of Wisconsin law professor named Asifa Quraishi, which utilized Islamic precepts to point out the grave errors in the currently drafted law. In *Her Honor: An Islamic Critique of the Rape Laws in Pakistan from a Woman-Sensitive Perspective*, Quraishi tries to debunk the idea that Islamic law demands Zina (adultery/fornication) prosecutions in the form in which they have been legislated and enforced in Pakistan, reframing the Islamic law as a tool for women's empowerment rather than oppression. In addition to Quraishi, I also discussed the work of Quranic scholar Amina Wadud, whose *Inside Gender Jihad: Women's Reform in Islam* had just been published, and who had in 2004 become the first American woman to lead a mixed-gender Islamic prayer service. Like Quraishi, Wadud argued that Islamic religious doctrine, interpreted for hundreds of years exclusively by men, had to be reclaimed by women. In this reclamation lay the possibilities of equality and empowerment. I wanted to bring these women into the conversation, highlight the things they had to say, and perhaps even inspire my professor to use some of their work in the seminar.

In response to the paper I submitted, my professor was predominantly concerned that I had not engaged the texts that had formed the bulk of our class discussions. It was true. Those texts had overwhelmingly approached sex through the idea of pleasure and individual choice. I didn't yet have the tools to dissect these beliefs to underscore how they reiterated colonial condescensions. Indians had been too licentious then; they were too backward and unliberated now. I had tried to prove many things with the paper, primarily that sexual liberation was crucial, but not the sum total of empowerment. Instead of stating my arguments in the language of sexual consumption or delivering a Muslim vagina monologue, I wanted to make room for a feminist discourse that actually had relevance to Muslim women. And I was rejecting the premise that sexual pleasure had to be the centerpiece of feminist agitation.

My professor's lack of interest in Muslim feminists is an example of how ordinary instances of overlooking, sidelining, and ignoring work accumulate to ensure the larger project of marginalization and erasure. Even today, when the work of Black or Brown or Asian or Muslim feminists is included in gender studies classes, it is likely to be offered up as a condiment, the entrée being the white feminist texts. Where are the gender studies courses that teach predominantly the work of Black and Brown feminists?

The same mechanics of exclusion and erasure reappear at the activist level. Black feminist and scholar Treva Lindsay has critiqued the way in which the history of anti-rape activism in the United States, for instance, is told as a white feminist story beginning in the 1970s.[25] Yet anti-rape activism by Black women began in 1866, when a group of African American women testified before Congress about being gang-raped during the Memphis riots. Despite their courageous testimony, Congress refused to punish the perpetrators. In the later nineteenth century, Black feminist activists Ida B. Wells and Fannie Barrier Williams founded and participated in anti-rape campaigns. Much later, in the final quarter of the twentieth century, Black women were finally joined by white women, who were just waking up to the necessity of campaigning on the issue and had until then not made alliances with Black women. Despite the fact that Black women had been working on the issue for a century, it was white women whose interest is recorded as seminal in most feminist textbooks and discussions.

In a more recent example, articles and discussions surrounding the #MeToo movement often leave out the fact that it was founded by a Black woman named Tarana Burke (and not Meryl Streep, Alyssa Milano, and their celebrity cohort) in 2006. And little attention is given to the fact that in 2018 Burke criticized the #MeToo movement for ignoring the concerns faced by poor women in favor of those of white celebrity women. In a keynote address at the "Facing Race" conference, Burke tried to convince her mostly Black and Brown audience to recommit to the movement: "The No. 1 thing I hear from folks is that the #MeToo movement has forgotten us," she said of Black, Hispanic and Native American women. "Every day, we hear some version of that. But this is what I'm here to tell you: The #MeToo movement is not defined by what the media has told you. We are the movement, and so I need you to not opt out of the #Metoo movement. . . . I need you to reframe your work to include sexual violence. That's how we take back the narrative. Stop giving your power away to white folks."[26]

———

When I was taking that grad class in feminist theory, few feminists were questioning "compulsory sexuality" or the push to understand everything about gender identity and gender relations through the rubric of sexual orientation. I first wrote about it for *The New Republic* in 2015, and even then it was still a relatively new idea. When that article went online, I received many letters from women, most of them Brown, who ardently agreed and told me how they had been waiting for such an argument.

Undoubtedly, the message was not a new one in more conservative countries like Pakistan, where the sexualization of Western societies is routinely critiqued and held up as a symbol of moral decay. But what I was saying was different; it did not come from a place of faith but rather from one that saw the limits of the transformational power of "sexy feminism" in a society where sex had been thoroughly co-opted by capitalism. And it identified the white feminist catch-22 that any critique of compulsory sexuality coming from a Brown Muslim woman was likely to be discarded as an expression of some latent discomfort with sex itself. I was criticizing the loss of feminism's power to take on capitalism.

A month before *The New Republic* article went to print, *New York Times* columnist Michelle Goldberg noted that: "For a lot of people, the contemporary sexual regime celebrating pleasure over all else isn't that much fun." Goldberg was discussing the work of Rachel Hills, an Australian feminist who spent several years documenting the consequences of sexual liberation for Millennials; having sex, even a lot of sex, she argued, had become its own oppressive sexual convention. Hills argues that "true female sexual autonomy doesn't just necessitate the right for women to have sex without stigma or judgment, although this is important. It also entails the right to confidently not have sex when it is unwanted or unavailable on the terms she might prefer."

Hills presented findings from the hundreds of interviews she had conducted, many of them stories of women who felt that they had to pretend to be more sexual than they were in order to fit into the ideal of the cool, hip feminist. Magazines like *Cosmo* and others marketed to women bolster this paradigm, pushing the achievement of orgasms, adventurous sex lives, and the constant incorporation of novelty as the basis for a good and even healthy sexual life. All of this, Hills concludes, has led to the transformation of women from sexual objects to sexual subjects. While the former were policed by other people, the latter police themselves, watching and regulating their own behavior in order to create for themselves an identity that fits the cultural ideal.

The co-opting of Western feminism by capitalism

through the Trojan horse of sexual liberation can be witnessed anew as it turns its attention to queer culture. Concepts like sexusociety and compulsory sexuality are useful here not simply to point out the universal expectation for feminists to have sex and the tyranny of that pressure for asexual women, implicitly closed out of feminist acceptance. They also show how late capitalism continues its work in the name of "sexual liberation" to commodify new sexual orientations. Once sexual orientation is essentialized and defined, it is then reborn as a market category of people to whom particular things can be sold. Freedom, even sexual freedom, then, is reduced to the freedom to consume and perform, not justice or equality or redistribution of resources. For political movements centered on these latter issues, the realm of possibility is submerged and subsumed by the commodifying capacities of capitalist enterprise. Recognition of LGBTQI identities has come to mean not just equal rights within legal systems but also marketing to those who belong to them. Equality also means corporate recognition and the development of a consumerism centered on the purchase of products tailored to particular sexual identities as a form of empowerment.

One example is the transformation of Pride festivals into consumerist extravaganzas of rainbow-emblazoned products. As a 2018 article from *Wired* noted, "everyone," particularly large corporations, wants to get in on Pride now.[27] Target sells "Love Wins" T-shirts, Nike sells "Be True" sneakers, and Burger King even introduced the "Proud Whopper" in some major metropolitan markets. Apple also got into the game recently, selling the Pride edition Apple Watch wristband, and the energy drink Red

Bull set up billboards that showed a row of cans in rainbow colors and the slogan "Wings for Everyone."

The sale of these products is not bad in and of itself, particularly to the extent that it normalizes LGBTQI identities and promotes inclusion. The danger is that consuming such products becomes the primary way that people engage with these identities, ignoring the histories of draconian oppression and exclusion that LGBTQI individuals have experienced in a prejudiced culture and the work that still needs to be done in so many communities to ensure basic acceptance and safety and equal rights for these groups. In the words of one critic, "Did Marsha P. Johnson and Sylvia Rivera take on the cops at Stonewall to sell T-shirts?"[28]

The central question to ask about "rainbow-washing" and its older cousin, "pink-washing," which sees everything splashed with pink during "Breast Cancer Awareness Week," is whether the radical potential of these freedom movements is curtailed or co-opted by corporations through the popularization of products tailored to women or LGBTQI identities. When sex sells in a society based on buying and selling, then everything is about sex and buying and selling. Politics, particularly the politics of an intersectional feminism that is truly accepting of and inclusive to LGBTQI individuals, must be committed to the goal of justice and equality beyond just the free expression of sexual orientation.

Sex has always been central to the ways in which white feminism holds white women apart from—and above—women of color. Black women are held up as dangerously sexual to a deviant degree, too primal in their expression of their sexual needs and desires to be cute role models. (Note there is no Black character in *Sex and the City*.) If white women's sexual liberation is something to be celebrated, Black women's sexual liberation is a danger to the system, something to be tamed and brought within the bounds of white-defined decency. A 2018 National Women's Law Center study found that Black girls "face adults' stereotyped perceptions that they are more sexually provocative because of their race, and thus more deserving of punishment for a low-cut shirt or short skirt" and that "Black girls are 17.8 times more likely" to be suspended from DC schools than white girls. One reason for this disproportionate punishment is that adults often see Black girls as older and more sexual than their white peers, and so in need of greater correction."[29]

If Black girls and women are too sexual and don't cover enough, Muslim American girls, including those who are Black, are seen as covering up too much and are asked to remove their headscarves. One Black Muslim athlete was disqualified from her high school volleyball match because she refused to remove her headscarf.[30] Another was asked to remove her hijab and prove her religion.[31] A Muslim woman at the Black Lives Matter protests in Michigan following the murder of George Floyd was similarly forced to take off her headscarf by the Detroit police, who incorrectly alleged she had to take it off for her mug shot.[32]

If sex-positive feminism imposes behavioral norms on women in America, it similarly expects that women elsewhere in the world state their goals and aims in the same language, equating liberation with sex positivity. The stories and narratives of the "other" that get touted as heroic and worthy of alliance must similarly invoke this language, the centrality of sexual pleasure, as the essence of feminism and the pursuit of it as its central tenet. It is not a benign request.

Corporatized feminism's project of depoliticizing feminism has been aided by the emergence of strains of feminism that are not judgmental at all about the substance of women's decisions or even concerned with their political import. "Choice feminism" is a term coined by philosophy professor Linda Hirshman, who used it "to name the widespread belief in the US that the women's movement has liberated women to make whatever choices they want."[33] While Hirshman focuses on the choices women make about wage work and unpaid labor in the home, choice feminism is now a much broader phenomenon.

Choice feminism (like sex-positive feminism) responds to criticisms of feminism being too radical and too judgmental by offering no criticisms of any choice at all. Essentially fearful of politics, choice feminism does not challenge the status quo, celebrates women regardless of the choices they make, and abstains from any form of judgment of their actions—even if damaging to other women—altogether.[34] Beyond its problematic satisfaction with the status quo, choice feminism allows women to avert the difficult decisions of making the personal political: demanding change from friends, family, and lovers. In making everything feminist, it essentially ensures that nothing is feminist, nothing requires change, nothing requires a sacrifice of individual self-interest for the collective good.

Judgment, exclusion, and calls for change are unavoidable parts of politics. If feminists are not to withdraw from political life altogether, they must acknowledge the difficulty of engaging in politics. Political claims are partial; but it is in their partiality that they present the possibility of transformation. The idea that contestation of any and all sorts is bad, has been instrumental to the depoliticization of politics.

Both sex-positive feminism and choice feminism minimize and sideline the concerns of women of color and poor women who need the status quo to change. In this crucial sense, then, choice feminism prioritizes the needs and beliefs of white feminists based on individual choice because constructing a collective and engaging in the very political processes of consensus-building and contestation of various claims is not suitable for their purposes. Ironically, "choice" feminism actually ensures that those who are not benefiting from the status quo—from the untrammeled exercise of power and individuality that comes with white privilege—will never have choices beyond those they have at the present moment. In this crucial sense, then, choice feminism is white feminism. It is incontrovertible that women should have the ability to make choices, including sexual choices, and have complete dominion over their bodies, free from state intrusion. At the same time, defending the ability of women to make choices need not mean an abandonment of critique of those choices to build a politically meaningful movement. It is also essential that the freedom to make choices does not get reduced only to choices pertaining to sex. A woman's ability to make choices must always be protected; so must the feminist project of challenging these choices when they obstruct possibilities of anticapitalist empowerment and political solidarity.

I wish I could have written all this for my graduate seminar. I had broken every gender norm I had been raised with, had chosen education and independence—and all the struggles that came with it—with little support. The seminar's preoccupation with sexual pleasure instead of sexual politics seemed so disconnected from the feminism that I was trying so hard to model for my daughter. If only I could have known I was not alone, had been able to hear the voices of Muslim and other feminists of color like myself waging front-line struggles against terror, against religious obscurantism, and against patriarchal domination, but yet excluded from white feminist discourse.

Many years have passed since that seminar in the basement room, and I am more concerned than ever, as sex-positive feminism eviscerates critiques of imperial overtures abroad and encourages a deliberate deafness toward all other dialects of empowerment, only because they won't affirm that freedom, essentially and exclusively, means the freedom to have sex.

CHAPTER SIX

—

Honor Killings, FGC, and White Feminist Supremacy

At twenty-five, after being married to my husband since age seventeen, I ran away to a domestic-violence shelter. For months, I remained in hiding with my two-year-old daughter, afraid that my husband would kill me. All the other women at the shelter to which I had fled, many of whom were white and American, were in hiding for more or less the same reason.

If my husband, who is of Pakistani origin but had spent his entire life in the United States, were to have killed me, it would automatically have been called an act of "honor killing," because both of us were Muslim. The Human Rights Watch definition of honor killing states: "Honor killings are acts of vengeance, usually death, committed by male family members against female family members, who are held to have brought dishonor upon the family. A woman can be targeted by (individuals within) her family for a variety of reasons, including: refusing to enter into an arranged marriage, being the victim of a sexual assault, seeking a divorce—even from an abusive husband—or (allegedly) committing adultery. The mere perception that a woman has behaved in a way that 'dishonors' her family is sufficient to trigger an attack on her life."[1]

My death would have met these criteria. At the same time, so would the deaths of any of the white women I met at the shelter who faced the prospect of intimate-partner violence because they had left a man or pursued a new relationship or had damaged the ego of some man in their lives. Honor and ego, no one seems to have noticed, are iterations of the same forces of patriarchal dominance. "Honor" makes sense to those in a collectivist society, "ego" to those who live in individualist one. Honor killing and ego killing are identical in their motivations to discipline and destroy women. The driving force in either case is a man who believes he is entitled to power over a woman's life.

The HRW definition does not prescribe that honor killing is specific to people of color. That is an implicit white assumption. A label of honor killing would never be attached to any of the thousands of white-on-white cases of intimate-partner violence. It is the presence of a Black or Brown male perpetrator that fosters the idea that a crime is determined by the cultural or religious identity of those involved.

To go back once again to the British, the agenda of colonialism involved manufacturing definitions of new crimes and new classes of criminality to make a point about the moral degeneracy of the people whose freedom, goods, and land were being looted. This was central to the civilizing mission of the colonizers.

As Bernard Cohn has documented in his book *Imperialism and Its Forms of Knowledge*, the British ruled by creating the ethnographic state, which meant they collected all and every form of data surrounding Indian life, practices, ethnicities and so on.[2] They could tell Indians "facts" about themselves based on the data that they had collected. Some of the data was for benign purposes, but in other cases it was used to set different groups against each other. As the British East India Company became a colonial administration, the traditional systems of law, such Qazi courts or even grassroots institutions for dispute resolution such as village councils, found their power eviscerated. British-imposed conceptions of criminality (unlike the old traditional ones) tended to be impersonal and divorced from the intimate contextual knowledge that the former had possessed.[3] In addition, convicted Indian criminals from this era, whether they were male or female, were often transported to other parts of the empire as indentured labor, thus solving the empire's labor issues.[4]

In the mid-nineteenth century, abortion and infanticide were classified as crimes in India, and Indian women became a new class of criminals. According to these rubrics, Indian women were baby killers worthy of enslavement in one instance, but hapless, oppressed beings that could only be saved by the British in others. The larger idea was to disrupt existing norms and mores and interpose colonial denominations in their place. The 1837 debates on the establishment of a Uniform Criminal

Code in India emphasized that "even while there were no laws on abortion in England, the proposed criminal code must have laws against foeticide because of its widespread prevalence in India where illicit sex led to illegitimate pregnancies."[5] The premise that there were no laws against abortion in England was only partially true; the Ellenborough Act of 1802 did criminalize abortion, but the law was rarely enforced, with later statutes even creating an administrative option in which defendants were charged with "concealment of birth" rather than "criminal abortion" or "murder of an unborn child."[6] Conviction of the lesser offense was in fact common in suspected infanticide cases during the nineteenth century, since English juries were notoriously averse to ever handing down the death sentence that a murder conviction would entail.[7]

In Britain at the time, sex outside monogamous marriage was considered just about the biggest threat to a socially ordered society. The social and legal ramifications for a woman found guilty of adultery were harsh, far-reaching, and usually irrevocable. So there was no reason to believe that British women were not conducting covert abortions where necessary to conceal those illicit couplings just as frequently as Indian women were. The likelihood of being charged with the lesser offenses detailed above were not included in the Indian discussion of the matter. Whether or not they may have been concerned with abortion in India itself, the white colonizers were clever enough to realize that painting Indians as inveterate baby killers was an ideal way to construct the colonized as criminal and hence to strip them of their humanity.

In India, "infanticide" became a means to specifically

prosecute women. The despicable crime of infanticide itself had long existed, but the practice of charging women for it began under the Infanticide Act of 1870, after which deaths of female infants could be attributed to men but the deaths of all male babies invoked prosecution of the mother.[8] That is, for any cases in which a male child was killed, "the new innovation lay in the shift in culpability" from male leaders to women.[9] The rendering of what was a complex situation into a singular apportioning of blame was what distinguished colonial law from customary practices. Unlike in Britain, women in India were actually convicted of infanticide. In April 1881, a Brahmin widow named Vijayalakshmi, aged twenty-four, was sentenced to death for killing her newborn illegitimate infant.

The British had an ulterior motive in prosecuting Indian women for infanticide. Many of the women convicted of the crime but not sentenced to death were transported as indentured labor to other colonies.[10] By the 1880s, the majority of convicts transported to Southeast Asia from other parts of the empire were women convicted of infanticide, and reports from the time suggest that four-fifths of all women imprisoned in India had been convicted of killing their own babies.[11] Once they were transported to other British settlements, they were used as domestic forms of labor, notably cleaning, grinding grain, and sewing. Since most transported convicts were men, these same women were later also held responsible for the emergence of "vices" such as prostitution arising in the settlements.[12]

Unsurprisingly, equivalent infanticide cases were given completely different treatment back home in England. In the late 1880s the widow Esther Bishop was tried for infanticide in Colchester. Her baby had been found dead in a laundry copper filled with water; the postmortem investigation suggested strongly that it had been born alive and had subsequently been drowned. The jury convicted Bishop of "concealment of birth." This was typical of conviction patterns for infanticide cases tried in England at the time; the majority were settled with a conviction based on a lesser offense.[13]

Infanticide was a horrendous crime, but in the application of the statute British judges and magistrates did not account for the specific conditions of the women coming before them, or the fact that for many the choice was to keep the baby and die oneself (without any way of guaranteeing that their illegitimate baby would be cared for) or live themselves and have the baby die. Even as they adopted the rhetoric of saving Indian women from barbarous men, they demonized the same Indian women suffering the consequences of sexual double standards and patriarchal control, alleging that Indian women were so prone to promiscuity and illegitimate sexual relations that they required harsh and particular punishment.[14]

White colonizers manufactured similar moral panic in response to the practice of "sati," or as Europeans called it, widow-immolation. (In Sanskrit, "sati" refers to the woman who dies, not the ritual, but because I am primarily referring to European accounts I will use "sati" to mean the ritual.) The rite—which was not strictly a religious practice—involves a Brahmin widow casting herself on her husband's funeral pyre, and it was rare in India even at the time. Large parts of the country did not practice the barbaric ritual at all; in other regions, it was restricted to certain castes. In the seventeenth century, when the British first encountered sati, witch-hunts, trials, and burnings were still being conducted across Europe and in the American colonies.[15] Yet despite the many similarities in the "spectacle" of burning women, and the purportedly moral underpinnings for doing so, white people apparently only recognized violence against women when it was perpetuated by what they saw as primitive "other" cultures.

Refusal to recognize British cultural brutalities stood in parallel to the refusal to recognize the brutality of colonialism itself. The European "Age of Discovery" required such claims of moral supremacy in order to justify colonial expansion and control. It did not matter that poor and largely powerless women at home in Britain could be subject to torture and then being burned alive at the stake with a cheering audience from the village in attendance, nor that the practice of sati was at least in some cases nominally consensual, arguably a tiny step more shocking than the very non-consensual process of witch-burning. The Indian ritual was primitive and extremist and its European counterpart was a normal part of the maintenance of order.

To underscore this point, the British set about trying to prove not only that sati was a prevalent and integral part of Hindu culture but that it must be banned on humanitarian grounds. They searched for evidence of the practice in Hindu sacred scripture, combing the five-thousand-year-old Vedas (by no means easy, as they were not properly codified given the oral culture of the time) until they found a single reference that corroborated their own assumptions about sati, its religious character and its inhumanity. Thus they combined three imperialist moves: turning Hinduism into a monolithic religion based on scripture (which it was not); deciding which pundits' interpretations to accept as legitimate (crowning themselves the final arbiters of "correct" Hinduism); and writing into historical existence a "tradition" of sati (which remains highly debatable).[16]

Contemporary accounts of the act were penned by zealous British missionaries (few natives, let alone outsiders, had ever even seen it happen), and then regurgitated by future travelers. These accounts are transparently motivated by constructions of the racial other as "fundamentally incapable of providing either 'normal' emotional relationships or physical safety from sickness, violence, and even death without the benefit of Christian and in particular British interventions."[17] Gleefully dramatic reports such as this one about a fourteen-year-old widow, published in *London* magazine in 1827, were often recycled again and again: "She soon leaped from the flames and was seized, taken up by the hands and feet and again thrown upon it much burnt, she against sprung from the pile running to a well hard by laid herself upon the water course weeping bitterly. At length on her Uncle swearing by the Ganges that if she would seat herself on the cloth (that he provided) he would carry her home, she did so and was bound up in it and carried back to pile now more fiercely burning and thrown upon the flames."[18]

The British passed legislation criminalizing sati in 1829. It was one of the very first statutory interventions that the British made in India and the egregious barbarity of the practice duly emphasized the "moral" case for imposing colonial laws as the British presence transformed from a trading partnership into an occupation.

Conveniently, around this time sati narratives began to include the British intervention and its positive effects. In 1829, William Bowley of the Church Missionary Society described an account of a sati in which he intervened and asked the widow, "Why do you destroy yourself?" to which she responded, "My Thakoor" (lord and husband), pointing to her husband's corpse. Bowley then tells her, "This perishing corpse is not your Thakoor nor do you have any relation to him now that he is dead. He came into the world alone and is gone alone." Bowley manages to convince her to let her husband be burned on the pyre and postpone her own burning till the next day. Overnight, Bowley tells his readers, he makes sure to have the widow guarded by Muslim police officers because he distrusts Hindus who could drug and kill her. In another conversation the next day, the widow confesses to Bowley that "all are her enemies" among her community. Bowley, the hero, is now able to procure her rescue: "I told her that if none of her relations would protect her, she might send to me and I would see that justice was done her. I also got the Police Officers to offer their services in the event of being oppressed and she was somewhat eased."[19]

Demonizing Hinduism as morally inferior to Christianity, sensationalized narratives of sati remained in circulation throughout Europe for decades to come. So crucial was sati's position in the British imagination that an account of it even appears in Jules Verne's adventure *Around the World in Eighty Days,* published almost fifty years later in 1873. In the novel, the protagonist Phileas Fogg encounters the practice deep in an Indian forest. His travel companion explains that a woman is shortly to be burned alive: "And, if she were not, you cannot conceive what treatment she would be obliged to submit to from her relatives. They would shave off her hair, feed her on a scanty allowance of rice, treat her with contempt; she would be looked upon as an unclean creature, and would die in some corner, like a scurvy dog."[20] In the "sati" of British colonial imagination, Hindus were cast as hypnotized by Brahmanic texts and hence incapable of disobeying them.

As theorist Gayatri Chakravorty Spivak pointed out in her analysis of sati, the British saw highlighting and then abolishing the practice as part of their civilizing mission in India; they would "save" the native women. In contrast, Hindu men alleged that the women wanted to die. Thus two patriarchal systems, with white men on one side and Brown men on the other, erased the woman and there is "no space in which the sexed subaltern can speak."[21] Testimonials from Hindu women further call into question the religious basis of sati, suggesting that the concerns of widows were predominantly material and social, and not religious.[22] The widows could not remarry, and if they did not have children (or even if they did) they had few means of supporting themselves or even protecting themselves from sexual violence, illegitimate pregnancies, and so on. In some areas, such women, presenting a threat to the domestic order and fidelity of husbands, had to live on the outskirts of villages with no social structures to support them. Sati was a rare response to an impossible situation, yet the white colonial conception of religion as "the structuring principle" of the Hindu society left no room for a wider consideration of the material hardship and social dimensions of widowhood.

The modern phenomenon of honor killings in Muslim communities is also closely connected to the colonial interventions of white British occupiers in India. Precolonial Islamic jurisprudence and judicial practice involved a panoply of Qazi courts, all following different religious schools of thought, belonging to different sects, and thus often coming to different rulings on the same question. These included the four main Sunni schools of thought and two Shiite, all with different views on different subjects, including interpretations of the Quran, the Hadith (traditions of the Prophet Muhammad), and everything else. This intentional plurality of religious conflict resolution reflected a plurality of practices among the Indian Muslim population, and provided that population with plenty of opportunity to shop around and take their case to the court that seemed most appropriate to their own practices and beliefs. It was a dynamic and responsive justice system that reflected the realities of daily life and evolved with the times. Its growth and evolution was in fact a crucial essence of how law itself was conceptualized. In this sense, the Islamic legal system when it existed was the opposite of British law, built as it was on stare decisis, or the upholding of calcified precedents indefinitely into the future.

The earliest records of the British establishing their own courts in India date back to 1726, when the East India Trading Company established mayors' courts in Madras, Bombay, and Calcutta.[23] By 1786, circuit courts had been established, followed by subsequent reforms that gradually replaced the British version of codified Hindu or Muslim law along with British Common Law. Prior to this, neither Muslim nor Hindu law was codified. The British eviscerated the extant pluralistic system of justice when they began to codify it by rolling everything into a single statute that was said to represent a majority of Indian Muslims. Islamic law, with its permissive forum-shopping, its openness to interpretations by various Qazis (judges), was inherently unsuited to codification, whose entire purpose was consolidation into singular laws and meanings.

Even after the British Empire disintegrated, the legacy of this rigid perspective on one unified "Islamic law" persisted. Qazi courts were interconnected with (though not entirely dependent on) the Mughal and the Ottoman Empires, both of which were defeated by the British, whose legal system gradually replaced them. Today, Qazi courts, some informal and others state-sponsored, do exist in some parts of the world, but none are in the form in which they existed before the British colonization of India and the sectioning off of the Ottoman Empire. The consequence of using this one-size-fits-all model is that judges have little or no license to consider the individual circumstances of each case. And this in turn leaves the law open to abuse by bad actors. The problem was not with the statutes themselves but rather that the statutory form itself was the incorrect method of codification in that it precluded the possibilities of varying schools of thought and interpretations of issues in favor of the one that was recorded as the statute. One example of this can be seen in Pakistan's 1990 "Qisas and Diyat Ordinance," which allowed family members of the deceased to pardon a murderer from his or her sentence after the payment of "blood money."[24] The law does not exclusively apply to honor crimes, but its existence often makes prosecution of honor killings difficult. This would have been a good idea in a more pluralistic judicial system, where courts were able to consider the relevance of financial reparations for a crime on a case-by-case basis. This possibility, which would have allowed precluding cases that involved an honor killing or suspected honor killing, was not provided by the statute. The Qisas and Diyat Ordinance, whose intent is to provide monetary reparation to the victim's family in exchange for the perpetrator's freedom would no longer be a loophole for honor killers.

But the legal consequence of applying the law indiscriminately was that it opened up a loophole to be exploited by the perpetrators of honor killings. When spousal homicide occurs, for example, other members of the family (since perpetrator and victim often belong to the same family) could step in and forgive the killer, hence erasing the crime itself. Anti–honor killing statutes in Pakistan have tried to undo the loophole but have had little or no success because murderers insist that the crime was not actually an honor killing (and hence an exception to the blood-money law) but simply a garden variety murder.

Honor crimes are one of Western journalists' favorite subjects when reporting on the Muslim world. The assumption is that telling these stories somehow works to end honor crimes in general, ensuring the safety of others who defy their families by raising the profile of the issue, putting it onto the international agenda. But the fact that honor killings are still occurring in Pakistan, drawing protests in Jordan and rising in India, suggests this premise is faulty at best, actively misleading at worst.[25] On the other hand, it is easy to see how such storytelling benefits the white Western journalists who engage in it (leading to the same kind of financial and reputational gains discussed in Chapter 4), and how it reassures white Western readers and "saviors" of their own good fortune.

Any honest analysis of honor crimes would need to consider the social and material circumstances that foster intimate violence against women—in hundreds of thousands of cases of male-partner violence in the United States and United Kingdom, as well as in foreign lands. To take the example of Afghanistan, we need to begin by acknowledging a society whose familial and institutional structures have been broken by five decades of Soviet and U.S. foreign intervention. Romantic marital "choice" is unavailable to nearly anyone, male or female, in Afghan society. Instead, marriage is generally seen as a means of cementing frayed communal relations in a war-torn land.

In Jordan, the fight against honor killings has focused on a repeal of a law exempting from penalty men who discover wives or female relatives committing adultery, and who may have killed or injured one or both of them.[26] Repealed in March 2017, the law that had been on the books was actually taken from the Syrian Penal Code, which in turn is based on the French Napoleonic Penal Code, which shaped development of laws throughout the Middle East and North Africa.[27] It was the French, then, who instituted leniency in cases of honor killing, while also giving it the charming nickname of *crime passionelle*.

The Jordanian reforms from March 2017 also did away with the "fit of fury" defense—comparable to the "heat of passion" defense permissible in voluntary manslaughter cases in many jurisdictions of the United States—which mitigates punishments in honor-killing cases. (Judges are still permitted to consider pleas by the victim's family for reduced sentences for the perpetrators, who are often from the same family.) The irony of what was done in Jordan, a country that had been considered by Human Rights Watch to have a high rate of honor crimes, is that similar provisions continue to remain on the books in the United States. In many U.S. jurisdictions, murder defendants may invoke the "heat of passion" defense, whose validity is judged by similar criteria as the Jordanian law and, if accepted, means more lenient penalties.

The heat-of-passion defense requires an inquiry into whether the defendant was "obscured" or "disturbed" such that a reasonable person, sufficiently provoked, could act from passion rather than judgment: the most common example being the sudden discovery of spousal adultery. Some jurisdictions apply the standard of "extreme emotional disturbance," which downgrades the charge of murder to manslaughter if there has been extreme emotional disturbance for which there is reasonable explanation, again such as discovery of a woman's infidelity.

All of these defenses help to exonerate male perpetrators of violence against women. Legal scholars have noted that the substance of heat-of-passion defenses is similar to those offered up by domestic abusers who batter their wives.[28]

Westerners read honor killing as endemic to "foreign" cultures and proof of their particular barbarity while continuing to permit heat-of-passion defenses for certain murderers at home. Violence against women in "other" countries is an indictment of religion, culture, and the particular depravity of the people, while the same violence in the United States is considered an aberration, particular to the individual who commits the crime, rather than to a nationally endemic pattern of misogyny and toxic masculinity. But acknowledging that "honor killing" is comparable to violent crimes perpetuated against women everywhere in the world would cast into doubt one of the main moral edifices of the imperial endeavor. It would necessitate the sort of scrutiny of the violence of white men in which white patriarchal powers have no interest. Instead, "honor killing" must be an incomprehensible, exotic phenomenon driven by mysterious cultural imperatives.

Like the nineteenth-century preoccupation with Hindu sati, twenty-first-century Muslim honor killings must be seen as uniquely evil in the eyes of the West. Yet not only does this characterization demote feminists of color as passive, unable to curtail their uniquely violent men, it also does a tremendous disservice to white women, obscuring the true extent of the poison of gender-based violence and its tacit acceptance by legal systems rooted in English Common Law and the Napoleonic Code.

Certain "cultural crimes" (honor killings, female genital cutting, child marriage, and so on) are now set apart from universal, "normal" crimes by the implication of a wider cultural complicity in non-white cultures, because indigenous feminists of color failed to eradicate them. White women, the superior feminists, we are expected to assume, have been able to transform their culture in a way that these other women have not. Yet given that the moral architecture of colonialism depends on the casting of the native as morally inferior, it is essential to question those assumptions. The very idea of cultural crimes specific to native peoples, and laden with a specifically heightened moral disgust, allowed colonists to paint local populations as inherently morally abject. Thus coercive and exploitative colonial intervention could be recast as a benevolent and necessary civilizing presence.

———

Like sati and honor killing, the practice of female genital cutting fosters moral outrage in which the West stands on the right side and anyone trying to introduce the complexities of the issue into the debate is discredited as a secret supporter of the practice. Likewise, there can be no nuance in the discussion—for instance, questioning whether the practice of a small nick or cut for cultural or religious rituals not wildly distinct from the traditional practice of a bris for male Jewish infants is the moral equivalent of full clitoridectomies. Nor is the epidemic of privileged American teenage girls cutting themselves generally seen as a symptom of a barbaric culture in the same way. And even though the practice involves a tiny percentage of Arab and African women, President Trump and his allies used it to call out feminist opponents of the Muslim ban, like Elizabeth Warren, as hypocrites.

In her essay "Who Defines 'Mutilation'?" Courtney Smith challenges the "hegemony of Western feminist discourse" surrounding female genital cutting (FGC) by conducting an analysis of what a group of Senegalese women thought about breast implantation versus what a group of

American women thought of FGC.[29] The comparison is directed at pointing out how much cultural frames influence our judgment of various practices (and *not* toward creating equivalence between a harmful practice carried out on minors versus one that is usually chosen by adult women). As Smith describes it, both groups were a bit confounded by each other's choices, American interviewees seeing FGC as a "castration of women" and an effort to "keep them down," and Senegalese women saying about breast implantation that "no man would want his wife to do that." But there were also women in both groups who could see the other's perspective. One American interviewee observes, "When I think about it, plastic surgery is kind of similar to genital cutting. Sort of like, you are cutting your body to fit a mold, to define who you are through physical attributes. A lot of women who are older get botox—they want to be attractive and beautiful and young again. Who told you that that is how to do it?"[30] Similarly, a Mandinka woman interviewed in Douba in Senegal said, "In Senegal, excision is similar to breast implantation because something is changed or taken away from the woman in both of them." Even more interesting was the statement of a development worker who was engaged in spreading information about the adverse health consequences of FGC who said, "If there are health consequences, there are health consequences. There aren't Western consequences and African consequences and there aren't American women and African women. There are just women whose bodies are being transformed."

Other scholars, like the anthropologist Saida Hodzic, have pointed out how the Western zeal for manufacturing "modern" African subjects often lies behind the discourse on FGC, promising/positing that the elimination of FGC would make African countries like Ghana (where Hodzic did her research) fully modern. One of Hodzic's discussions with a representative of a reproductive-rights NGO in Ghana illustrates the misunderstandings that define Western vehemence on this score. This particular NGO had been in charge of providing "sensitization" training on FGC. Included in the training are questions like "Why Call it female genital mutilation?" and the answer "The World Health Organization has a definition and we all must use it."[31]

Pushing this kind of "sensitization" training, Hodzic says, requires NGOs to desensitize themselves to the actual needs and views of rural communities so that they can push a paradigm and moral binary that is not based in their reality. When she meets Olivia, an NGO worker, a member of the Ghana Women's Welfare Association who works directly with rural populations, and asks her about the biggest problem facing women in poor and rural parts of Ghana, Olivia immediately responds with "economic problems." Women like Olivia, however, have few options because donors prefer funding educational workshops rather than the redistribution of material resources. One NGO, "Rural Help Integrated," chose to pursue a "holistic" approach and ordered a millet-grinding machine for use by the rural women—a decision questioned by a United Nations Population Fund, who asserted that there was no connection at all between reproductive health and the machine. According to Hodzic, "Had rural women been included in the conversation, they would have vigorously disagreed." The machines greatly reduced the hours the women had to spend manually grinding millet, allowing them to rest and regain their strength, thus ensuring better health outcomes.[32]

As Courtney Smith writes at the end of her parallel study of Senegalese and American women encountering each other's views on FGC and breast augmentation, it is crucial to create dialogue between cultures. She advocates for "the possibility that we will learn from our encounters with other human societies to recognize things about ourselves that we had not seen before."[33] Dialogue occurs when both sides of a conversation feel that they are, at least to some extent, on *equal* ground. The enduring frame of white saviordom, and the belief that white Westerners are in charge of eliminating practices like FGC, makes it nearly impossible to inhabit this kind of conversation.

One example of the ways in which this racist framework blocks meaningful communication and progress is seen in Sara Johnsdotter's study of compulsory genital cutting cases of Swedish-African girls.[34] Sweden was the first country in the world to criminalize FGC in 1982, and has been extraordinarily interested in cracking down on parents suspected of continuing the practice since then, even though the number of cases in Europe as a whole and Sweden (and also the home countries of most of the suspects) are very low.

According to a law passed in Sweden in 1997, a girl or young child can be subjected to a genital exam without the knowledge and permission of the child's legal guardian if they are suspected of having undergone FGC. Looking through police files of 122 FGC cases, Johnsdotter found numerous examples of incorrect reporting. In one case, a teacher noticed that a six-year-old child in her class was taciturn and secretive after a visit to Somalia. She immediately reported this as a suspected FGC to the authorities. The parents, afraid of being prosecuted, agreed to an examination. Two gynecologists who examined the girl found that her labia minora were missing. The prosecutor was willing to press charges, but when the girl was examined again by a pediatrician, that doctor pointed out that the child's labia were completely intact. The prosecutor was so incensed that he accused the parents of having taken a different girl to the exam.

In another case, Johnsdotter reported, a father was nearly sent to jail because his daughter had had a car accident in which the genitalia was outwardly damaged, and subsequent surgeries made one of the nurses suspect that FGC had taken place. The racism and xenophobia in these compulsory exams and the racist inability of Swedish doctors to tell the difference between one or another Somali child is simply accepted.

A 2018 study of FGC in Africa shows that the numbers of girls/young women who underwent the procedure have fallen from 71 percent to 8 percent in the past twenty years, owing largely to the work done by indigenous African women.[35] Countries like Sweden, the United States and the United Kingdom, however, continue to use the practice as a means of typecasting migrants traveling to and from Africa.

In 2016, Immigration and Customs Enforcement (ICE), in collaboration with the U.K. government, initiated "Operation Limelight," an effort to crack down on

FGC at British and American airports. Designed by the Homeland Security Investigation's "Human Rights Violators and War Crimes Center," Operation Limelight seeks to "bring awareness to FGM and deter its practice by educating the public about the risks and penalties associated with it."[36] Conveniently, the data used by ICE relies on old studies and shoddy methodological procedures.[37] The statistics, which were referenced in the press statements about the initiation of Operation Limelight, all originate in a paper titled "Female Genital Mutilation/Cutting in the United States: Updated Estimates of Women and Girls at Risk, 2012."[38] The paper takes the number of female immigrants from various African and Middle Eastern countries and multiplies it with the rates of FGC prevalent in those countries to conclude that the risk of FGC in the United States had increased threefold since 1990, with more than half a million women and girls at risk.

Operation Limelight sets out a false imperative for intrusive examinations of African immigrants. According to an ICE press release, agents who have received FGC-related training are stationed at large airports, where they select individuals from "high risk" countries to provide with "informational brochures" about FGC, with the intention of deterring them from carrying out "vacation cutting" (taking girls to receive the procedure in countries where it is legal). In another press release, the modus operandi seemed a bit clearer: "Agents engaged approximately 700 individuals in the international terminal destined for Dubai, Addis Ababa, Ethiopia, Cairo, and San Salvador. Approximately 40% of passengers were traveling with children. Flight crew and airline employees in the international areas were also provided materials for additional outreach."[39]

These interactions may seem innocuous to non-immigrants, but they can be fraught experiences of powerlessness for immigrants who likely have no option but to answer the questions posed by ICE officials, do not know if a physical examination is forthcoming, and also do not know whether the exchange will have immigration consequences for them.[40] Understanding the terror of these interactions requires that white women get past their own privilege and learn to empathize with women who do not have the power to say no to such intrusions.

Few details exist of what sort of questions are asked of these people or the fear among girls and women that they will have their genitalia examined by ICE agents. ICE is, however, quite proud of having won the "World Class Policing Award"; a photo from the event, held in London, shows four white people beaming as they hold the award they have won for their alleged concern for the health of African women and girls.[41] Meanwhile, needless to say, the affected communities were not consulted or involved in determining what programs would be most effective in bringing about desired change.

The fact that these programs are not community-generated or -directed means that the level of intrusion that is considered acceptable in policing against FGC is never passed through any sort of community consensus, let alone consent. Anyone who is Muslim or Black or Brown or Somali, who may critique this sort of airport thuggery by ICE officials allegedly "protecting" the genitalia of Brown and Black girls, is automatically tossed into the pile of secret supporters of the practice. Since the culture that permits FGC is itself considered bad and community members automatically complicit unless they insist otherwise, it is only ICE agents of an increasingly white-nationalist state who can do the job. It is important to note that there is no public-health dimension to this intervention. If it were truly a concern about minor girls being forced into this practice, an appropriate agency to be tasked with the matter would Health and Human Services, not Immigration and Customs Enforcement. The possibility of the practice thus becomes the basis of racial profiling and demonization of immigrants from certain countries over others.

There is no clear evidence of what exactly ICE was doing with FGC suspects, but there are cases of alleged forced hysterectomies performed on migrant women in detention. Exerting dominion over Black and Brown bodies to instigate fear in female migrants and asylum-seekers, the Trump administration weaponized a contemporary version of the forced genital examinations carried out by British administrators in the Indian colonies. Officially, ICE is authorized to test for STDs among detainees. In late summer of 2020, a whistleblower at the Irwin Correctional Facility in Ocilla, Georgia, filed a complaint with the Department of Homeland Security, ICE, and the warden of the Irwin County Detention Center (ICDC), about an unusual number of hysterectomies being carried out on the center's detainees. The procedures were allegedly performed outside the facility, at the nearby Irwin County Hospital, on immigrant women, many of them unable to speak any English, who did not authorize their surgeries with proper informed consent; rather, they were treated as if communication was unnecessary. When they awoke, many were confused about what had been done to them. Neither was it easy to figure it out.

On October 21, 2020, an independent medical review board tasked with looking into the allegations found "a disturbing pattern" in which women were being pressured to have gynecological surgery.[42] They said it was possible that the ICDC was complicit in what was happening, referring women to the gynecologist even when they did not have gynecological complaints. The staff required women who were resisting the surgeries or exams to have psychiatric evaluations. The review board's analysis of the medical charts of the detainees found a lack of adequate documentation of their histories, their level of comfort with gynecological exams, and most of all their need for surgery. "Surgery," the board wrote, "was overly aggressive without any demonstrable medical necessity."

For its part, ICE has set about deporting the women who have made the complaints in an effort to delegitimize their claims. After all, if the women are not able to provide interviews and participate in the court process, ICE can proceed with their cover-up. According to a Columbia law professor working on the issue, the speed of deportations has increased following President Trump's defeat in the 2020 election, and ICE is actively destroying evidence so that its illegal procedures are not questioned.[43]

It is worth remembering that forced hysterectomies have precedent as recently as the 1970s, when Latinx women in Los Angeles were forcibly sterilized because they were held responsible for the increasing population.[44]

Like the Indian women who were all labeled prostitutes and the Namibian women who were made subject to genital examinations by British colonial authorities, officers from ICE and detention staff see migrant women as less than human. The old patterns of domination do not disappear with time.

The story about forced hysterectomies at the Irwin County Detention Center broke the week before the death of Justice Ruth Bader Ginsberg on September 18, 2020. While the death of the justice provoked debate among white feminists about the future of reproductive rights in the United States, almost none connected feminist organizing around reproductive rights to the forced hysterectomies allegedly being carried out at the behest of the American state on minority women in captivity. Amid all the discussion about bodily freedoms, the use of state power to prevent women of color from reproducing was somehow lost.

White women's "feminist advocacy" around "cultural" crimes like honor killing and FGC actually compounds the injuries done by the crimes themselves in stripping their survivors of agency. In addition to suffering the cruelty and depravity of the crime, local women find themselves devalued or silenced by foreign "saviors" who see them as victims unable to advocate for themselves. In aid contexts, feminists of color must follow the lead of programs and advocacy plans led by white women if they are to access funds that permit them to work on the issue. At the same time, others in their communities might perceive them as beholden to white feminists, and thus anti-culture/anti-tradition because of their exclusive focus on crimes.

At American domestic-abuse shelters, first as a resident and then seven years later as an attorney working at a different shelter in the same area, I could not help but notice that there was no white abuse or Brown abuse or Black abuse; it was all just abuse. The same despicable taxonomies of misogyny, entitlement, and dominance appeared again and again in abusers' language and in their behavior. Women who dared go against their partner, or any other abusive family member, were afraid for their lives, just like I was. They worried about custody of their children, the future beyond the shelter, the economics and the logistics of surviving while always looking over their shoulder.

The rhetoric around violent crimes, just as in the sphere of international development, of war, of sexual freedom, celebrates white women as having gone further in their battle for equality than feminists of color have. This hierarchical relationship with women of color suits the interests of white men, whose violence is seen as qualitatively different from and superior to the violence of people of color. Meanwhile, white women who imagine themselves terribly lucky not to fear honor killings or FGC can imagine that the crimes committed against their bodies are somehow less of a cultural and social problem than those committed against Black or Brown bodies. Thus divided, white and non-white feminists are much less likely to create trouble at home or take collective action against patriarchy at the global level.

The hope for change has to come from discarding such hierarchies. It must come from building collective organizations that can resist the pressure placed on vulnerable and traumatized women to act as proof of white feminists' superior enlightenment, empowerment, and international status. Only then can feminists attempt to create the dialogic spaces in which solidarity can flourish. Only then will it be possible for women to work with one another, to discern what is universal in the issues that confront them and to realize the possibilities of cooperation.

—

CHAPTER SEVEN

"I Built a White Feminist Temple"

In 1979, poet, feminist, and civil-rights activist Audre Lorde addressed New York University's Institute for Humanities Conference. In her speech, titled "The Master's Tools Will Never Dismantle the Master's House," Lorde had asked: If white American feminist theory need not deal with the differences between us, and the resulting difference in our oppressions, then how do you deal with the fact that the women who clean your houses and tend your children while you attend conferences on feminist theory are, for the most part, poor women and women of color?[1]

The cult of individualism, and the resultant form of feminism made notorious by women like Facebook executive Sheryl Sandberg in *Lean In*, and to some extent by Gloria Steinem before her, encourages every woman who reaches power to believe she got there on her own and without any free passes. The suggestion that racial privilege may have played some role in her rise, that white men are more willing to cede power to white women, is an intolerable threat to this mythology of the self-made superwoman. Late capitalism's individualist reading of success is very much a part of the American dream of self-improvement through hard work—promoting the illusion that the system is fair and rewards effort in a linear and consistent way, rather than driving productivity to the disproportionate profit of already-wealthy white men.

As they themselves benefit financially, white feminists, in their own lives and careers, have managed to ignore the realities of what we now call intersectionality.

In 1989, Kimberlé Crenshaw, then a law professor at Columbia University, wrote a groundbreaking critique of three court decisions on Title VII (anti-discrimination) cases, in which she showed that within existing legal frameworks, Black women could only be protected from discrimination to the extent that their claims aligned with either Black men or white women.[2]

In *Moore v Hughes Helicopter*, the issue came down to whether a Black woman could claim to represent all women in the way white women did when alleging discrimination under Title VII.[3] Moore, the plaintiff, had alleged that her employer practiced race and sex discrimination by not promoting women and Black employees to senior positions. At trial, her attorneys introduced statistical evidence that showed that there was a significant disparity between men and women in promotions and Black men and white men. Moore was asking the court to certify "Black women" as a class so she could then pursue a discrimination case on their behalf. The court refused to do this and the case went up to the Ninth Circuit Court of Appeals, which held that because Moore had asked for class certification on behalf of "Black women," there "were serious doubts as to her ability to adequately represent white female employees." In other words, white women could represent discrimination against *all* women, but Black women could not. This was because when white women alleged gender discrimination, it was a pure gender claim, unlike when Black women represented all women.[4]

In her analysis, Crenshaw pointed out that Black women such as the plaintiffs were located at the intersection of both racial discrimination and gender discrimination. To limit them to legal consideration within just one of these categories denied the plaintiffs equal justice with individuals who occupy just one protected class, because it did not make any attempt to understand the particularities of their position. Crenshaw wrote that no justice could be done to Black women, or any women of color, if it did not consider both race and gender in its analysis. She called this idea "intersectionality," explaining that "the intersectional experience is greater than the sum of racism and sexism, any analysis that does not take that into account cannot sufficiently address the particular manner in which Black women are subordinate."[5]

Crenshaw's analysis did not just take legal theory to task when she exposed the conceptual limits of single-issue analysis; she emphasized the necessity of transforming existing systems of power at every level of society. She recounted the experience of Black feminist activist Sojourner Truth when she addressed a women's rights conference in Akron, Ohio, and famously asked "Ain't I a Woman?" Many white women present wanted her to be silenced because she would draw attention away from the cause of suffrage and toward the cause of emancipation from slavery. Crenshaw's point was to underscore how "the difficulty that white women have in sacrificing racial privilege to strengthen feminism renders them susceptible to Truth's critical question. When feminist theory and politics that claim to reflect women's experiences or speak to Black women, Black women must ask 'Ain't We Women?'"

Adding Black women on as appendages to systems that have long excluded them and calling it "diversity" is not the answer. Building on the work of earlier Black feminists like Audre Lorde, Crenshaw's focus is on how minority women suffer at the hands of a system that was never made to accommodate them or has no capacity to make them whole. "These problems of exclusion cannot be solved simply by including Black women within an already established analytical structure," Crenshaw writes, refusing to believe that the mere recognition of identity is the sum total of what a society and a state can do in response to discrimination.

In the thirty years since her seminal article was published, Crenshaw's conceptualization of structural inequality and systemic racism has become integral to understanding the experiences of women of color within a white-dominated world. In a 2005 article focusing on the complexities of intersectionality, feminist theorist Leslie McCall called it "the most important theoretical contribution that Women's Studies in conjunction with related fields has made so far."[6]

Feminist theorist Christine Bose has further expanded on the theory to note its relevance to feminists beyond the

United States, emphasizing that "U.S. scholars should not be surprised that an intersectional approach is useful to European, Asian, or African scholars studying inequalities in nations with diverse native populations or polarized class structures, or with increasing numbers of migrants and contract workers from other countries."[7] Scholar and author Momin Rahman has applied intersectionality to being queer in his crucial essay "Queer as Intersectionality: Theorizing Queer Muslim Identities."[8] Others are focusing on understanding intersectionality as a research methodology or as the basis for policy initiatives on gender inclusion.

And yet even as Black women apply intersectionality to understand their experience of discrimination, white women must analyze the other side of the coin: their experience of privilege. Discussion of the intersection of whiteness and womanhood remains a taboo, particularly when it prods at the complicity ordinary white women who have benefited from white privilege play in propping up a racist system. This is particularly true in the elite, professional circles where white Western women are most likely to identify as feminist but are so ensconced in their bubbles of privilege that they cannot make the empathic leap to consider that discrimination they don't see is real and has negative effects on the lives of others who do not enjoy white privilege.

Part of the problem, as Crenshaw shows us, is that "the authoritative universal voice, usually white male subjectivity masquerading as non-racial, non-gendered objectivity, is merely transferred to those who but for gender share many of the same cultural, economic and social characteristics."[9] In other words, white women take on the voices of white men and that is considered progress. Institutions that were once male-led and are now female-led continue to practice the same kinds of exclusions, derisions, and erasures. Yet everyone congratulates themselves on having chalked up a win for feminism, for all women.

Crenshaw's descriptions in theory match my own experiences in practice. The women I worked with while serving on the board of Amnesty International USA were familiar with feminist theory and how a male-dominated system encourages white women to reenact the same exercises of silencing and domination that they have themselves experienced. And yet it is still so tempting for white women to interpret their own ascent as a matter of pure merit, and their own quest for parity as the most urgent priority. It is so easy to be unconcerned with domination, silencing, and oppression when they are perpetrated on those you barely see. So effortless to replicate those unthinking, convenient sins as you forge ahead toward the glass ceiling, teeth gritted. Late capitalism's individualist reading of success is very much a part of the American dream of self-improvement through hard work promoting the illusion that the system is fair and rewards effort in a linear and consistent way. In reality, all of it is a ploy to drive productivity so that the white men at the top of the pyramid continue to get ever-wealthier.

As a consequence, white feminists have ignored intersectionality as it pertains to their own lives, careers and choices. Many white feminists are upset by the accusation that white women have largely upheld and endorsed the racial inequities that were in operation at a time when men dominated all and everything. Most, including the chairman of the board whom I served under at Amnesty International, would vehemently and passionately endorse intersectional feminism as a concept. But in practice, ambition, self-preservation, or the need to hold on to an ideology of self-made success seems to intercede. There is no ceding space or voice or power: feminists of color who want to function within this system must cater to white feminists and laud their ascent regardless of the situation of women of color.

Coming to understand Crenshaw's arguments has given me strength and purpose. And yet, throughout my years as a lawyer, as an activist, and as an author, I've had to question whether to continue to participate in white structures that prescribe a limited and tokenizing role for women of color. Like many other feminists of color, I have wondered whether these existing structures can be dismantled and remade from the inside or whether they must be abandoned altogether.

As we deconstruct various aspects of the feminist movement and expose the role of whiteness as a hegemonic, regulating force within feminism, the question still remains unresolved: should feminists of color construct feminisms of their own and forget about cross-racial solidarity, or should they persist within structures that are led by and tailored to the needs of white women?

"I built a white feminist temple and now I am tearing it down," wrote Black feminist Layla Saad in a blog post that went viral in 2018. In the post, Saad spoke about her experience of building a life-coaching business called "Wild Mystic Woman." Saad used solely Black women's imagery in her branding, and she, a Black woman, was ultimately in charge of things. Yet the truth, Saad confessed, was that she catered mainly to white women, not intentionally but by default. "The unintentional default in most online businesses (regardless of who runs those businesses) is that whiteness is centered. White imagery, white clients, white perspectives, and white narratives of success, empowerment and spirituality dominate this industry. This is because this industry reflects the white supremacy ideology that white is seen as 'universal' and applying to all, and non-white is seen as 'other' and applying only to those who are non-white."[10] Saad's confession was a commitment to do better, to "tear down the white feminist temple" that her endeavor had become. It signified that even with a commitment to racial and gender justice, it is most often easier to inhabit the systems that we find ourselves in than to dismantle them because of their inequity.

Many white women perform wokeness quite well, carefully asking for the correct pronunciation of your name in front of others and posting black squares on their social-media accounts on the one day when anti-racist activism becomes briefly fashionable. Even more are in the habit of appropriating the culture of Black, Brown, or Asian people to boost their own cosmopolitan credentials: Instagram grids awash with butter chicken and turmeric lattes, peppering their speech with "bae" and "twerk" and "fuckboy" and "basic"—all words appropriated from Black slang. But there is a sense in which the reverse is true. Brown and Black women also engage in adopting white standards in their own lives, and so are co-opted into the perpetuation of their own oppression. Sometimes they assimilate these beliefs from being constantly bombarded with them by cultural forces, while at other times they oppose them but do not feel safe in speaking out.

For white women, it is a matter of gilding their status. For women of color, it is a question of survival and not a choice. Whiteness confers power that can yield professional and personal success and generally make life far better than it could be otherwise. Many feminists of color have spoken out against white-centered feminism, but many more are caught in personal, professional, or economic circumstances too precarious to risk, finding themselves with no opportunities to confront the monolithic structures of white power or confront defensive white women who are more interested in feeling good about themselves than constructing a more egalitarian feminist conversation.

For example, a close female friend of mine who is a woman of color got a job at a fancy new startup that focused on developing a women's club geared primarily toward upper-middle-class and urban white women. My friend had a long and notably Indian name, so the CEO of the company, a white woman, started to call her by a shortened version that she (the CEO) devised herself. My friend complained about it to me, so I was shocked when, at a talk arranged by her company, the same CEO got up onstage and introduced my friend by her nickname and not her actual name. Then, when my friend took the stage, she, too, used the nickname to refer to herself. Not knowing how to correct her boss without jeopardizing her job, she had simply given in.

I've known of examples where white women college

professors in the United States have taught books that castigate Islam and demonize the veil, even when there were students who wore it in the classroom. Many of these students did speak out to other university officials, but the professor had tenure and so ultimately nothing was done. These sorts of interactions not only ignore the tremendous power difference between professor and student, it ignores the way power dynamics of whiteness within academia work to further delegitimize narratives from Black and Brown communities. The "white savior feminist" professor is in this sense a central culprit in pushing Western-centered narratives, not least the right of white and Western women to pass judgment on the rest of the world's women. Recognizing these power dynamics means that white feminists, used to privilege, experience a de-privileging of their perspectives, but meaningful allyship requires just this.

It's hard not to see the way things are as the way things will always be—and as soon as you start to believe that, speaking out against the million microaggressions or the many large ones becomes an act of pointless stupidity and self-sabotage. Better to be the good Brown or Black or Asian handmaiden of mainstream feminism, assuring white women that they are doing everything right, that complaints are the product of hypersensitivity or misunderstanding or jealousy—anything other than the dominant power of whiteness within feminism itself.

A few years ago, I was invited to lunch at the Women's Caucus of the Indiana General Assembly. When I arrived, my host requested that I address the gathered women about the issues facing women in South Asia and also about honor killings. Put on the spot in this way, I could not say no.

My audience's fervent questions and interruptions made clear that they were most interested in hearing about the honor killings. I spoke honestly and factually about the brutal details of these kinds of killings. While I tried to emphasize the complexity of the issue, I had not had time to prepare. So I did not address the ways in which honor killing is functionally equivalent to intimate-partner violence, or tell them that "honor" is a euphemism for the male ego, which is seen to act alone in America and in the name of the collective in Pakistan. I told the binary story of good and evil that they were expecting.

At the time I did not recognize the purpose of the event. I found out later that my host, an extremely well-intentioned, liberal feminist, had invited me to speak because she wanted the caucus, a mixed group of Republican and Democratic women, to have something that they could agree on. That something, she had decided, was a collective shudder and sigh at the terrible plight of foreign women who did not have their rights and privileges. It was the bipartisan issue that allowed white feminists of different political affiliations to speak to each other.

In retrospect, I made a bad situation worse by my cooperation. I did not know how to separate the facts of honor killing from the frame of white feminist superiority which they invited; I had actively corroborated the white women's stereotypes about Brown and Muslim women. The white feminists had ceded space, allowed me to speak, but only on the condition that I indict the culture of my birth, and affirm, at least indirectly, the supremacy of America, of white women, of Western civilization. It was a victory for white feminism, and I had enabled it.

It is not that culturally coded crimes aren't crimes. But there is a problem in so readily attaching a cultural dimension to intimate-partner violence that takes place in Brown and Black communities to indicate that it is somehow different or more brutal. Such attachments demand that feminists of color denounce their racial or cultural communities if they are to participate in feminist discourse. When Westerners focus on particular crimes in Afghanistan or Ghana, they create stunted forms of resistance where everything that is the focus of Western attention for "moral reform" is suddenly the most authentic expression of culture. Feminists in these communities get branded as agents of the West, and indigenous cultural opposition that would have castigated honor crimes or FGC are destroyed when the calculus becomes the Rest against the West. This then fosters a narrative in which white and Western cultures are amenable to feminist transformations while endemically barbaric Black and Brown cultures perennially lag behind them. If there is no parity between feminists who are having the conversation, gender parity as a whole becomes an unreachable goal.

—

CHAPTER EIGHT

From Deconstruction to Reconstruction

In June 2020, while I was writing this book, *The Daily Beast* published an in-depth report of racism within the National Organization of Women (NOW).[1] NOW is America's oldest and largest feminist organization, with 600 chapters across all 50 states.[2] It is a very white organization: 17 of 27 board members are white, and 10 of 11 presidents have been white.[3] One of its case studies was the organization's 2017 leadership election, which included an all-women-of-color ticket for the first time in NOW's history. China Fortson-Washington, an African American woman, ran for president, with Monica Weeks, a young Hispanic feminist, as vice president on the same ticket. But in the weeks of their campaign, they faced noticeably more hostile audiences than any previous candidates, or indeed than their opponents in that year's race. Speaking at the Brevard, Florida, chapter, Weeks was heckled for saying that as the most oppressed women of color, disabled LGBTQI people needed to be given a voice to make everybody better. A white woman inter-rupted her, saying, "White women too," and "yeah don't forget the white women," and another yelled, "Only the women with pussies." No such interruptions or heckling took place when white women were speaking.

That same June, Fortson-Washington addressed the audience at NOW's annual convention as part of their bid for president and vice president. Even before they addressed members from a stage, they were getting racist pushback from one NOW member to "tone down the His-panic a little bit." Others dismissed Fortson-Washington as "angry" and Weeks as a "hot-headed Latina."

When Fortson-Washington took the stage, the racism was even more obvious. As soon as she began to speak, her white opponent, seated onstage, took out her laptop and began to type. It was an extraordinarily rude and dis-missive gesture designed to undermine not the points her rival was making but the fact of her very presence onstage, the likelihood that she had anything of value to say at all. Fortson-Washington had not done any such thing when her opponent had been speaking. In the audience, a woman said audibly to her friend, "Just because she is Black she thinks that she would be a good leader?" Another complained about "all this Black Lives Matter crap." When it was time for questions, Fortson-Washington and Weeks were asked what white women were supposed to do if everyone was focusing on Black women.

It is not only NOW that has had problems with race. In July 2020, the *Lily*, the *Washington Post*'s feminist-oriented online magazine, published a report focusing on three major feminist organizations in America: the National

Organization of Women, the American Association of University Women, and the Feminist Majority Foundation. In their interviews with twenty staffers, *Lily* reporters found a landscape where racism was rampant. Staffers of color said that they were concentrated in the lower levels of the organization, with white leadership shaping organizational priorities that felt irrelevant to women who are not white, straight, cisgender, highly educated, and upper-middle class. Employees of color were often made to feel like "tokens," many told the interviewers, rolled out to show diversity but dismissed within the confines of the office.

In June 2020, Toni Van Pelt, the NOW president who had demeaned China Fortson-Washington onstage, was removed after increasing allegations that she sidelined women of color. The new president installed in her stead was Christian F. Nunes, a Black woman. When interviewed about whether her taking the helm would produce any changes, Nunes said, "I thought I was really going to be able to help this organization, but ultimately I feel like I have just been a token."[4] She added that when she called out the racism at NOW, she was kept out of executive meetings, with her duties reassigned to white women.

The Feminist Majority Foundation, which notably supported the invasion of Afghanistan in order to "save" Afghan women by occupying their country, has its own problems. Sherill Dingle, a Black woman who worked at FMF from 2017 to 2019, reported that when staffers brought up instances of racism, the president, Eleanor Smeal, would deflect by reminding everyone of her own participation in the civil rights movement, and that she had marched with Coretta Scott King (the wife of Martin Luther King Jr.).

Conversations about race, Dingle reported, often turned into "screaming matches." Five other staffers from FMF verified Dingle's statements. One of them, Shivani Desai, who had worked at FMF during the same period as Dingle, noted that Smeal had "particularly volatile reactions to young Black women" and would pointedly try to highlight various oppression experienced by white women, interjecting into conversations about women of color by saying, "and white women, too."[5] Smeal even complained about the 2016 exit polls that showed 53 percent of white women voted for Trump, claiming that number was "fake."

Other actions taken by Smeal showed a pointed disregard for her own white privilege. When the Trump administration implemented its "Zero Tolerance" policy of separating children from their parents at the U.S.–Mexico border, Smeal announced that FMF would take immediate action. In order to raise awareness, the staff of FMF would all get arrested and then released. She told her staff that she had already arranged with the police the conditions of their arrest and release. "This makes absolutely no sense," Dingle remembers thinking of the plan, the likes of which she had never seen in her career in organizing. Dingle refused to attend the protest, feeling unsure that she, a Black woman, would be treated the same as all the white women. For this, she faced reprimands from her white manager, who said attending the protest was part of her job.

"They didn't know their privilege," says Dingle. "Do you really think I can go to the police right now and say,

'Hey I'm trying to do a march, I need to be arrested and let go.' Do you honestly think that would go well for me?"[6] In another conversation in which Dingle tried to explain the experience of Black women, Smeal insisted that white women feel "powerless" or "unable to speak up" and fear they may be harmed because they are women. It was only later, when FMF was contacted for the *Lily* report, that they said, "We agree that Black women experience more oppression and discrimination than white women. Black women experience racism, white supremacy, sexism, patriarchy, and misogyny. White women experience sexism, patriarchy and misogyny." Even in their clarification they failed to understand that it was not a competition of relative oppressions, or to recognize that white women always possess white privilege and Black women never do.

At the AAUW, Raina Nelson kept suggesting research initiatives around the challenges faced by women of color. Her proposals never went anywhere, as the organization chose to focus its major initiatives on issues most relevant to white women. It was particularly frustrating for Nelson to be a part of the research team and see just how much AAUW focused on salary-negotiation workshops, which are largely irrelevant to women who work minimum-wage jobs. When Kimberly Churches, the chief executive at AAUW, was contacted about the organization's failure to fund research around issues important to women of color, she forwarded two articles in response; one was 300 words long and the other (a blog post and not a research project) was 700 words.

The *Lily* report also discusses how the white leadership of these organizations, particularly NOW and FMF, tend to support each other against allegations of racist conduct. Since board members of both organizations tend to be white and older, many are friends and form their own cliques on the boards. Eleanor Smeal and Teri Van Pelt (when she was still president of NOW), who are good friends, appeared at meetings together and backed each other's ideas before staff.

It seemed that not much had changed in the nearly four decades since Audre Lorde excoriated the National Women's Studies Association for their blindness to the injustice imposed by race. "I cannot hide my anger to spare you guilt, nor hurt feelings, nor answering anger; for to do so insults and trivializes all our efforts. Guilt is not a response to anger; it is a response to one's own actions or lack of action," she said.[7] Then, just as now, the United States was threatened by racial strife and the rise of a rabid right-wing politics. The white women Lorde spoke to considered themselves allies to Black women, just as many well-meaning white women do today. And like white women today, they were largely unconscious of the many injustices they inflicted on women of color.

Lorde listed some that she had personally endured in her speech that day. There was the woman who came up to her and said, "Tell me how you feel but don't do it too harshly or I cannot hear you." And the woman who, having just listened to Lorde read her poem about her anger, got up and said, "Are you going to do anything with how can we deal with *our* anger?" Finally, the time when the Women's Studies Program of a Southern university invited her to read following a weeklong forum on Black and white women. "What has this week given to you?" Lorde remembers asking the audience after the reading. At this, "The most vocal white woman says, 'I think I've gotten a lot. I feel Black women really understand me a lot better now; they have a better idea of where I'm coming from.' As if understanding her lay at the core of the racist problem."

The first all-women-of-color ticket for the presidency and vice presidency of NOW lost the election, but their candidacy did initiate an unmasking of the organization, exposing an internal culture of endemic racism. There was a mass exodus from the organization by those who disapproved of the way NOW had handled the issue of race. Tess Martin, a Black attendee at the conference, saw the hostility with which NOW members and leaders treated the first POC candidates for president and vice president of the organization. "NOW's true face is very different," she told reporters from *The Daily Beast*. "Below the convenient lip service to sisterhood, it revealed itself to be the worst kind of clique and the members are not women who look like me."[8]

"The war we are in is a war for narrative," Kimberlé Crenshaw told Abby Disney in an interview in June 2020.[9] To create an egalitarian feminism excised of the dominating agendas of whiteness, all feminists, and particularly feminists of color, must reshape the story of the movement such that the role whiteness has played in its development is made visible. We must end the celebration of feminist "heroes" who have propped up white supremacy, past and present, as we too prop it up by failing to speak out against them, by acting under racist assumptions or in complicity with racist practices and structures. Both NOW and FMF are membership organizations whose membership is by and large white. The difficult work of feminist solidarity happens when this demographic fact is *not* used as an excuse to focus solely on issues facing upper middle-class white women and map their concerns onto everyone else.

Scores of feminists of color, including me, still believe that this is possible. This is not an elimination of white women from feminism; it is an elimination of "whiteness" from feminism, in the sense that whiteness has been synonymous with domination and with exploitation. And this goal can never be achieved without the support of white women.

———

The justice system is inaccessible to millions of people because of the economic inequalities baked into our capitalist economic model. And poverty, along with many related issues like job insecurity, housing insecurity, educational disadvantage, and worse medical outcomes, disproportionately affects people of color. If race and gender directly determine an individual's treatment in our society, so too does class. I learned just how heavy the impact of class really was when I was a shiny new lawyer just graduated from law school.

After I passed the bar, the first job I took was as an associate attorney with a small African American law firm, owned entirely by Black attorneys and a staff made up mostly of persons of color. The firm specialized in civil-rights litigation, which includes Title VII cases of employment discrimination and sexual harassment. Young and idealistic, I considered the content of the job (if not the pay) to be a dream. Not only was I working for a majority-minority firm, but I would be helping those who had been discriminated against on racial or religious grounds. This kind of work was exactly what I had envisaged when I began training as a lawyer, years before. The firm was tiny and there was no empty office for me, so they set me up in the library ready to receive clients, and the clients came.

In one case, a young Hispanic woman employed in a local warehouse described how her coworkers would constantly make sexual comments, rub up against her, and even try to pinch her breasts. In another case, a woman who worked stocking the shelves at her grocery store was being harassed by a fellow employee who kept making lewd comments when no one was around. A white woman who worked at a convenience store came in alleging that she had been assaulted on the job by a fellow employee who was off the clock.

All this took place in just my first few months of working at the firm. Each time, after writing down the details of the case, I would tell the client to expect a follow-up call confirming whether the firm could take her case. The next morning, I would meet with my supervising attorney to go over the facts of the cases. I soon learned that it was not the client interviews but the post-briefing meetings with my supervisor, that would dissipate my idealism. In that first terse chat, and many thereafter, the senior lawyer would ask me: How much proof did she have? Did she know of others who had suffered similarly? Did her employer have a sexual-harassment policy that was posted in a visible location or in a handbook available to employees? Had she complained to a supervisor? Did she have a copy of that complaint? And, crucially, would she be able to pay costs?

If there was proof—a cell-phone recording, a couple of coworkers willing to corroborate and testify to having heard or seen something, or, better still, to being harassed themselves—and if there was no sexual-harassment policy or designated Human Resources officer, then things were looking good. If the complainant had the capacity to pay at least a little bit toward the legal costs, we would have had a done deal.

Most of my clients could not pay, not even a little bit. And civil-rights cases usually involve large costs, not only in terms of attorney time but also thousands of dollars to pay for transcripts of depositions and experts. There are costs associated with the filings themselves, costs associated with arranging and paying for video depositions in which the defendant can be questioned on the record with the statements serving as proof admissible in court. Experts are indeed very expensive and often necessary to prove, for example, the post-traumatic stress that often resulted from harassment and discrimination. Attorneys' fees themselves can theoretically be waived until an outcome is reached, but the rest are up-front costs that require immediate cash flow.

The practice of contingency fees means plaintiffs do not have to pay until there is a payout from the defendant being sued, and the intention is to make sure that anyone, particularly those who do not have the thousands of dollars to pay for up-front costs, can afford to pursue justice. Our firm had a tight budget (my desk was in a corner of the library and some clients "worked off" their bills by filing and making copies) but we did in theory take cases on contingency. We would not reject clients because they could not pay these costs, but we would accept them a lot faster if they could.

That first woman's case, the warehouse worker experiencing sexual harassment, was not, on its face, strong. The legal elements were all there, but there was little corroboration; she did not know of any harassment policy, but I suspected one would be fished out when her employers heard of the complaint. When she returned a few days later, I had to give her bad news. There would be significant difficulties in pursuing the case and likely high costs involved. Would she be able to pay? The answer was no.

The impact of class is further inflated if a person belongs to a racial minority. Twenty-one percent of all Black people in the United States live below the poverty line, along with 17 percent of Hispanics and 24 percent of Native Americans/Alaskan Natives.[10] In contrast, only 9 percent of whites live in poverty. The further below the poverty line that one falls, the greater the likelihood of experiencing "deep poverty," where one's earnings are less than half of the poverty-line number. Forty-four percent of those below the line are estimated to be in "deep poverty."[11]

According to the Center for American Progress, women of all races have higher rates of poverty than men across all races and ethnicities. Twenty-three percent of Black women live in poverty, along with 17 percent of Hispanic and nearly 25 percent of Native American/Alaskan Native women.[12]

These numbers are important because they represent the extent of the problem. According to the statisticians who put together the numbers, one of the primary reasons women of color fail to get out of poverty is the failure of economic redistribution mechanisms such as government programs for food stamps, welfare benefits, subsidized housing, and so on.[13] The importance of improving these increasingly neglected programs cannot be underscored enough; they must be revamped and improved if women of color are to achieve parity.

Similar circumstances prevail in the United Kingdom. The recent implementation of benefit cuts and austerity measures have pushed an estimated 14 million people into poverty.[14] Black and Asian households in the lowest one-fifth of incomes have seen a 20 percent decline in their living standards.[15] A study on the impact of austerity led by women from communities in Manchester and Coventry found that 40 percent of African/Caribbean women, 46 percent of Pakistani women, and 50 percent of Bangladeshi women are likely to live in poor households.

These statistics reveal how gender justice provisions available through the legal system are most often needed by women of color who live in poverty. At the same time, within the American framework of sexual harassment and employment discrimination, there are few ways for these women to access the justice system and have their claims heard. The capitalist model means that even those law firms that offer contingency fees to their clients look at the issue from an investment perspective, determining whether their investment of a lawyer's time along with all the other expenses is likely to yield a profit for them.

In the case of the Hispanic woman who worked at the warehouse, the lack of evidence up-front meant that a just outcome was not guaranteed in her case, but the financial inability to have the case filed in the first place meant it would never come before a judge, never be heard or considered; a just outcome was absolutely impossible. This by and large is the situation of most BIPOC women who face race- and gender-based discrimination—they do not have any recourse.

In her book *Redistribution or Recognition: A Political-Philosophical Exchange*, critical theorist and political philosopher Nancy Fraser considers why redistribution is not usually included in discussions of oppression. Fraser focuses her attention on "the broad decoupling of cultural politics from social politics, of the politics of difference from the politics of equality."[16] Instead of simply taking "recognition" to mean "identity politics" or "redistribution" to equate to "class politics," Fraser takes her "paradigm of redistribution" to mean "not only class centered such as New Deal Liberalism, social democracy and socialism but also those forms of feminism and anti-racism" that look to fairer economic relations to bring about racial and gender equity and justice.

One of the impediments to gender justice is the unfortunate distance between "activist tendencies that look to redistribution as the remedy for male domination" as opposed to those that look "at recognition as a means of resolving gender difference." Politics focused on identity-based groups like gender, sexuality, religion, and race, tend toward demanding recognition. But the reality of people's material conditions, although often correlated with identity groups, nonetheless varies widely within each group.

In Fraser's view, "gender" is a hybrid category in which

women suffer both underrecognition and maldistribution. Gender justice requires both recognition and redistribution.[17] A recognition-and-redistribution-based approach would insist, for instance, that workplaces and educational institutions make special accommodations for women of color as a group and then ensure that they have additional rights that would ensure the financial support to help them reach gender parity. One literal iteration of this could be some form of free legal assistance to women of color who face harassment or discrimination in the workplace such that they have the ability to bring claims against employers. Others could be priority adjudication for women who face both race and gender-based discrimination at federal agencies such as the Equal Employment Opportunity Commission.

In her 1981 NWSA speech, Audre Lorde spoke to precisely this phenomenon.

> When an academic woman says, "I can't afford it," she may mean she is making a choice about how to spend her available money. But when a woman on welfare says, "I can't afford it," she means she is surviving on an amount of money that was barely subsistence in 1972, and she often does not have enough to eat. Yet the National Women's Studies Association here in 1981 holds a conference in which it commits itself to responding to racism yet refuses to waive the registration fee for poor women and women of Color who wished to present and conduct workshops. This has made it impossible for many women of Color— for instance, Wilmette Brown, of Black Women

for Wages for Housework—to participate in this conference.[18]

A hundred anti-racist conferences will do little good if the people of color they aim to empower cannot afford to be in the room.

Almost half a million people attended the Women's March in Washington, DC, in January 2017. The overwhelming majority of them were white, middle-class women. Teresa Shook, the retired attorney who came up with the idea for the march, wrote later that "the reality is that the women who initially started organizing were almost all white," and that she had initially called the march "Million Women March," a name that had already been taken by a large protest held in Washington, DC, in 1997 by Black women.

Aurielle Marie Lucier, writing in *Essence* magazine, talked about the passive racism she experienced at the march, from being pushed into a trash can by a "nasty woman" to being racially profiled by an elderly white feminist, and concluded that the white women had "marched for themselves alone." The emphasis on uteruses and pussies was also grating to Lucier, as it assumed that all women have them (thus excluding transwomen).[19]

Lucier was just one of the Black women who spoke out. Research on the environment before and after the march shows how Black commentators who were critical of the event were shut down. One of them, Bridget Todd, expressed fears prior to the march that marginalized women would be subject to arrest and actions by the police simply because the white women who had not voted for

Trump wanted to make a point. "I'm sorry white women some of you helped get us into this mess . . . perhaps it's not your voices that need to be amplified in the aftermath"[20] Todd received a lot of pushback for daring to say this, most of it underscoring the color-blind precept that the march was for "all" women. Todd was accused of "divisiveness, reverse racism and being angry at white women"[21] The war of rhetoric continued on the pages of the *New York Times,* where Emma Kate Symons wrote, "You are a woman and regardless of color and ethnicity and sexual orientation we should be one voice."[22]

It was just the sort of scolding that many women of color are quite fed up with; its central mistake not dissimilar to the preachy color blindness of critics of the Black Lives Matter movement who insistently use the slogan "All Lives Matter." It ignores the simple truth that those who benefit from their skin color cannot preach color-blindness, thus covering up their racial privilege.

The leaders of the march were proudly and publicly committed to an intersectional ideology, and yet they had not considered that Saturday, a day of rest for the middle classes, was just another working day for those in the service and hospitality industries—for cleaners, transport workers, carers, and those engaged in many other kinds of low-paid and often insecure work usually performed by people of color and immigrants. In 2020, the Covid-19 pandemic revealed that more than half of America's "essential workers"—including grocery-store clerks, janitors, and fast-food workers, generally paid minimum wage—are women, and of those women a disproportionate number are Black. Yet they were not seen as essential to the Wom-

en's March. So while many white women were attending the march on a day convenient to them, others, most
likely women of color and immigrants, cleaned their hotel
rooms, bussed them around town, and cooked the tacos
or noodles or pizza with which they would reward themselves after a hard day protesting injustice.

Intersectional approaches are hard work, but they are
possible. In the case of the Women's March, it would have
been useful to get the leadership of LGBTQI organizations
involved. Even more important, a good strategy would
have been to approach large corporations like Amazon,
McDonald's, Burger King, and so on, as well as major
hotel chains, to allow their employees to have time off for
attending the march. The fear of appearing anti-Women
could have been sufficient in many cases to ensure that
women of color had some opportunities to participate.
The march could also have created better connections
with the leadership of groups like Black Lives Matter so
that those affiliated with that organization had a visible,
agenda-setting role in the march.

Many of the white women who marched in 2017
wanted to show their political opposition to the election of
President Donald Trump. Yet even while they did so, those
who claimed color-blindness failed to acknowledge that for
Black and Brown women, the election of Trump presented
an actual threat. Even worse, they did not use the activism
of that moment to acknowledge the role white women's
support for white supremacy had played in the election. In
2020, when Trump lost, it was again revealed that white
women increased their support for Trump, with 55 percent
of them voting for the president's reelection.[23] The number

is particularly revealing because, following the 2016 election few white women (such as those quoted above) saw racism as a problem among themselves. It is also notable that more than 80 percent of Black women, the highest percentage by demographic, voted against President Donald Trump.

In subsequent years, the Women's March initiative has splintered into a number of separate organizations, each running its own demonstration on the anniversary of the original march. In 2020 there were questions about the continuing relevance of the march; some thought its goals, such as encouraging women to run for office, had already been accomplished.[24]

In the late 2000s, when I first started volunteering with Amnesty International USA, they operated something called the "own-country-rule" for country specialists. This meant I was forbidden from doing any work related to Pakistan simply because I was from Pakistan. It was a discriminatory rule that applied to immigrant people who may wish to work on their own country, but not to white people. The majority of white people worked on issues related to the United States all the time. The "gender" specialist worked on issues facing white women but also extended herself to other countries whenever she wished.

It was also a departure from the general white emphasis on expertise as qualification for all things. The consequence of the rule was that white people who were interested in working on a country, but who did not know the language or had never been there, were now the "experts," while natives of those countries who had immigrated to the United States could not apply/contribute their knowledge. Later on, as the rule became harder to defend, it was alleged that it existed to protect the volunteer from reprisals in their country of origin. (Volunteers could easily have made such assessments of risk themselves, given that all volunteer work on human-rights issues does involve some risk.) Brown and Black people were thus being excluded from policy discussions for their own protection. In 2009, when I was elected to the board of AIUSA, the rule had, after much urging, been changed.

However, there is an important distinction between what Nancy Fraser calls "affirmative change" and actual transformational change. The former is perfunctory, form-filling, intended to silence and appease; the latter requires the dissolution of underlying structures and hierarchies for a complete reformulation. Whether it is the National Organization of Women or an organization like AIUSA or even the Women's March, all require transformational change. This means reconsidering everything, from the way meetings are organized and conference calls are set up to the way public demonstrations are organized. The go-to for most organizations, sadly, is affirmative change: the installation of a Black woman at the top or the creation of a committee to look into "diversity" (AIUSA convened many of these, fostering the impression that something was being done, when all that was done was to establish another committee whose findings would not be available for months and sometimes years).

The change that we need, that feminism needs, is transformational change. The analysis of where and how to make this change must be intersectional, considering race and class and gender, and the redress must be both redistributive and recognitive. These are the demands of the moment but none of them can be met without a revival of the collective and, most important, a return to the political.

One afternoon in the fall of 2020, I had a discussion with an older white woman academic about a topic she considered terribly controversial and I not at all. The issue at hand was simple: during our conversation, I had confessed that I no longer used the "three or four waves" of feminist analysis in my writing and speaking about feminism. That structure, I told her, represented a way of looking at history primarily through the lens of white and Western women.

She was aghast. In her mind, my rejection of this particular historical frame, which is a mainstay in gender-studies courses all over the United States, was a precursor to turning all white women out of the feminist movement, even though they were not personally responsible or culpable for the wrongs of white feminists past, and even though they had, in her own words, "made the movement."

Her words, or rather her anger, have stuck with me. First, it is impossible for any change to occur unless white women, particularly older white women, let go of their paranoid belief that racial equality within the movement is some sort of surreptitious strategy to displace them.

Second, if feminism is to be redeemed, timeworn/outmoded/colonialist ideas of history, tradition, and contribution have to be transformed and new frameworks created to take their place. White feminists who lay claim to having "made the movement" are reflecting the structural privilege and power they have claimed at the expense of women of color. And as Kimberlé Crenshaw says, "The value of feminist theory to Black women is diminished because it evolved from a white racial context that is seldom acknowledged."[25] In order for any of these ideas to be of use to us, we need to face up to the environments in which they were generated. Creating a new narrative that is self-aware and unwilling to constantly repeat the injustices of the colonial past is essential to organizing women around the idea of solidarity.

Third, white feminists must recognize and understand the distinction between whiteness, whose inequities have left such rot within the innards of the movement, and being a feminist who is white. The former creates hierarchies that further entrench the race-based inequities in society and enshrines white culture, white ways—of eating, drinking, sleeping, speaking, communicating, and organizing—as "the" ways. The latter is a descriptive term unattached to an agenda of domination.

The difference is important; it refuses to allow white women to disengage from feminism under the pretext of being "banished" by an anti-white feminist agenda. When you are called out for white feminism, this is not a mere description of your racial heritage, something you may feel guilty about but can do nothing to change. It is a description of your words and actions. It is crucial that white women realize that being white and a woman are not the criteria that make a woman a white feminist; it is instead refusing to recognize white privilege. She can, instead, eschew territoriality and let go of individual egoism to help forge an authentically constructed solidarity.

Finally, white feminists must accept that true solidarity, where all races of women interact at a level of parity, means accommodating and valuing many different kinds of knowledge and expertise, first and foremost the kind that comes from lived experience. Accomplishing equality will require lifting up women who are not slick with jargon or rhetoric and venerating their contributions as much as those who know how to package themselves appealingly.

I began this book lamenting the evisceration of the "political" from feminism. "Empowerment," as I pointed out in Chapter 2, was a word coined by feminists from the global south and had collective political mobilization at its center.[26] Before its reduction to the mere economic process of handing out chickens or sewing machines or clean stoves, this idea of empowerment rested on three core components: power, conscientization, and agency. In the defanged version of empowerment that exists today, each of these components of empowerment has been redefined and repurposed: instead of power, women are given "livelihoods"; instead of conscientization of the structures of oppression, women are given leadership-skills training; and instead of meaningful agency, they are told to just lean in and push harder.[27]

The populist moment can also be a feminist moment, its possibility the reconstruction of feminism itself. But it requires solidarity to catalyze potential energy into meaningful action.

Solidarity, sadly, is easy to prescribe but far more difficult to actually create. You might think that "womanhood" is a fairly powerful shared "we" in itself, but it bears the taint of having meant "white women" and their interests and agendas from the days when Sojourner Truth asked "Ain't I a Woman?" to more recent events like the Women's March. Contemporary feminism is missing a clear political frontier toward which to unite; it cannot exist simply as a force in search of an inchoate equality or the undefined eradication of patriarchy. We must unite behind specific political claims, and perhaps the most important of those claims is that the dominance of capitalism is bad for all women, even white women.

Anticapitalist threads within feminism have historically been suppressed or inverted in order to protect the interests of white women, members of the richest race in the world. But the feminism that results—depoliticized, corporatized, atomized, affiliated with hollow consumerism or with violent domination—doesn't even serve the interests of those white women in the long run.

When every woman is individually "leaning in," no one is left to build mutual aid and support. And so the focus for each person is on conquering the system, just like white men have conquered it, rather than noticing the ways in which such conquest is structurally closed off to others around them. When you are pitted against an imagined "other" to win a still-miserly crumb of power, you do not pool knowledge with that other, you do not communicate about your different experiences, and you never build up a cumulative picture of the deep faults in the system itself. You never reach the point of questioning its very existence. This erosion of the collective impoverishes all women's lives, stunting networks of support, slowing the progress of rights and redistribution campaigns, and wasting enormous amounts of energy within feminist ranks on the continual fight for some of our number to be heard even amongst ourselves. Individualism is, in a very crucial sense, a building block of capitalism. One task that Helen Gurley Brown accomplished with the creation of the Cosmo Girl was to transform women into individualist and careerist economic producers who could be installed into the capitalist machine sated by the things they could purchase with the money that they made. For these reasons, capitalist forces have looked to depoliticize as many spheres of public life as possible. To create a feminist politics of solidarity, women have to recognize the forces that push them apart and push them into meaningless competition by keeping them from collective understanding and engagement. Individuality within the capitalist framework is an antidote to politics and solidarity.

The past forty years have seen the persistence of a neoliberal hegemony in all parts of public life. Around the world, people have been told that they have no choice but to accept the neoliberal consensus, which in turn has eviscerated the idea that politics can and must have a transformative component. Before the rise of authoritarians like Trump in America, Bolsonaro in Brazil, and Modi in India, politics seemed to have reached a point where there was no real difference remaining between the right and the left. Successive administrations in both the United States and the United Kingdom effected very little difference in policy, in the grand scheme of things. It's neatly summed up in Tony Blair's famous claim that "the choice is not between right-wing economic policy and a left-wing economic policy but between a good economic policy and a bad one."[28]

That incontrovertibly "good" economic policy, it turns out, was neoliberalism. But when political questions are reduced to mere technical issues whose outcomes are to be determined by experts, there is no space left for citizens to make choices about ideology.

Several decades of unchallenged neoliberalism has fostered a fear of the contentious and the political. It has also created a constant demand and elevation of technical, bullet-pointed "solutions" that suggest that complex policy issues can nevertheless be solved in a few easy steps and technocratic rearrangements. The NGO-ization of various political issues, such as the provision of services to women who undergo abuse or women who need legal aid, has taken these issues out of the arena of political contention. Waves of government defunding that have directly affected women are not even recognized as women's issues/feminist issues. When money for a grant that provides legal services to women in domestic-violence shelters is cut, it is difficult to even find out about it, so obscured are these decisions within layers of funding bodies and third parties, let alone to organize in resistance of those cuts. As with so many other formerly public goods, philanthropy unevenly tries to pick up the slack—but its priorities are shaped even more than those of government by the interests of wealthy white donors. A reconstructed feminism must go beyond the installation of women of color in key leadership positions in such charities. It must transform the very terms of leadership to move away from technocratic, politically "neutral" solutions and into the messy and vital arena of political contention. NGOs have a role to play in society, but the technocratic NGO-ization of the political space has left too many, particularly feminists of color, disenfranchised because of their inability to influence the agendas of these organizations. More attention should be given to activist organizations that can push for political change even if it means foregoing the tax deductions that accrue owing to donations in the former.

When everything is feminist, nothing is feminist. The we-can-all-agree-on-this brand of choice feminism has not only proven impotent, it has eluded accountability. After all, if everyone is responsible for ensuring an education for all girls, then no one is. This lack of accountability is why feminism has been reduced to a branding mechanism rather than a force for real change.

But giving feminism political meaning must not be conflated with exclusion. The definition of a feminist frontier as a line of political action and organization means that there will be women who fall outside it. But they will be women who disagree with its aims, as is their right, and not those who want to participate but find themselves in a devalued and persecuted identity category. The women who fall outside the group are not "excluded" in the sense of being devalued or ignored but rather women who for their own reasons make a political choice not to align themselves with the politics of feminism. To stand for something inherently means that some will choose not to stand with you. This is essential for the constitution of a movement, not a harbinger of its inadequacy.

—

On Fear and Futures

As I neared the end of writing this book, I was overcome with an acute sense of foreboding. Separating women into white and non-white means that many of those whom I love and respect could read my words as an indictment of themselves as "white women" as opposed to as friends, colleagues and family members. I recognize that this is both a reflection of our riven society and of the raw emotional contours that discussions of race incite in all of us. Recognizing this as the reality is the first step in considering how we move beyond calling one another out and toward a conversation that is urgent and necessary. If the Trump era has weaponized racial divisions to end conversation, my hope is to normalize the discussions so that we can move past being reactive and toward being transformative.

Toward this end, I have tried to construct an argument here for the possibility of seeing the world through the eyes of other women. This is an individual and collective challenge, and we must start from the understanding that this challenge is one that women of color have been undertaking for centuries, not out of any great compassion or racially inherent caring quality but out of the need to survive in a white-run world. It is time now for white women to meet them in this work and share the burden.

We must also realize that framing one another in the language of racial difference bears within it the possibility of turning away, of relinquishing others we have known and respected and loved because they belong to the opposite category of white woman or non-white woman. White women who have spent lives arguing and working to uplift the voices of women of color can feel as if they are being unjustly lumped with others who have racist views. Similarly, women of color can fall prey to overinterpretation or to ascribing racist motives even to overtures that are sincerely born of a desire for mutual understanding. I acknowledge these pitfalls because I have encountered and experienced them and also because I ardently hope that we, as women and as feminists, can get beyond them. I think it is crucial that discussions of white feminism not be understood as an indictment of all white women or a prescription to discard working across difference because racial difference makes mutual understanding impossible.

Writing this book has been instructive for me personally as to the emotional mechanics of race: the struggle to distinguish between what is genuinely part of the scaffolding of systemic racism and what is a reaction born of the trauma of exclusion. If white women must see beyond their own actions as individuals and to an understanding of power and privilege of the category that they inhabit, feminists of color must also reject the temptation to pathologize every flawed interaction. It is easy to be immersed in the paranoia that no sincere solidarity is possible and retreat to our own racial categories; it is much harder to relinquish the sense of being wronged and work toward coming together. I am hoping we can do this.

Critique is the first step in a long process of opening debate. Arguing for reinvigorating the possibility of political contestation necessitates that the ideas in this book be challenged and argued, be accepted or rejected without any interlocutors fearing being labeled as racist simply because they do not find them convincing or because they see alternative possibilities beyond the ones that are suggested here. It is my hope that in inviting this sort of critique and opening my own work to it that I can model its necessity. The history of systemic racism within feminism, some of which I have attempted to outline here, should not be a dead end to debate and contestation within feminism. White women must not feel that the critique of whiteness within feminism is some crude intimidation tactic meant to silence them altogether. Women of color should avoid using critique as self-defense against having their ideas and arguments challenged by feminists of any color, nor should they deploy it as a panacea against self-examination. If feminism and the feminist project are to be taken seriously in this moment of cultural transformation, this is absolutely essential.

This book is an argument for feminism to pitch itself against a very specific frontier, that of whiteness, where whiteness is not construed as a biological category but as a set of practices and ideas that have emerged from the bedrock of white supremacy, itself the legacy of empire and slavery. At the moment, that frontier cuts directly down the middle of feminism, making a true unified "we" of womanhood impossible, in part because we are unwilling to discuss and confront what whiteness has done to feminism, what it has stolen from it. But it can be cast out—through vocal and visible upheavals of structures of power. We must abandon the appendage style of inclusion, which assumes that the addition of one woman of color to your panel or your curriculum or your committee is enough. We must denounce those who continue to cling to exclusionary histories, stories, and forms even in the name of tradition. And the feminists who have too long used the privilege of whiteness to imagine a trickle-down feminism, its parameters defined from the top, must give way to feminists committed to punching up and dismantling the establishment.

Feminists today face the great challenge of transformation: an embrace of the adversarial while knowing that adversaries are not enemies, an embrace of community that does not require endless compromises by those with the least power, and a realism that accepts women as they are and where they are today. Prescient as ever, Audre Lorde knew this crisis that would confront us, the women of the future, when she wrote "without community there is no liberation, only the most vulnerable and temporary armistice between an individual and her oppression. But community must not mean a shedding of our differences, nor the pathetic pretense that these differences do not exist."[1]

———

When I look around me today, I see too many women of color turning away from feminism. In some cases, they are saying goodbye to mainstream white feminism in order to build more specialized movements: Muslim feminisms, Black feminisms, queer feminisms. These smaller groups have a powerful role to play, but we also need to create a space where different tribes can work together on issues that affect us all—and, vitally, where they can lend one another equally ardent support for issues that do not affect us all. Communities must remain free to have their own specialized groups, but that need not reduce their capacity or potential for coming together to create a potent and transformative mainstream feminist politics.

No movement that is unable to do justice amongst its own adherents is likely to accomplish any wider goals toward justice. This book has attempted to see clearly the different dimensions of the feminist movement as it exists today, how it has arrived at this point, and where it could go from here, such that every woman who calls herself a feminist, of any race, class, nationality, or religion, can see a path forward and a reason to stay.

ACKNOWLEDGMENTS

With deepest gratitude to Alane Mason of W. W. Norton, Hermione Thompson at Hamish Hamilton/Penguin Random House (UK), and Sarah Bolling of the Gernert Company.

NOTES

Introduction: At a Wine Bar, a Group of Feminists

1 Gayatri Spivak, "Can the Sub-Altern Speak?" in *Marxism and the Interpretation*, eds. C. Nelson and J. Grosberg (Urbana: University of Illinois Press, 1988), 271–313.

Chapter One: In the Beginning, There Were White Women

1 Bill and Melinda Gates, "Why We Swing for the Fences," *Gates-Notes*, February 10, 2020, https://www.gatesnotes.com/2020-Annual-Letter.

2 "Humanitarians of Tinder," https://humanitariansoftinder.com/.

3 Gertrude Bell, *A Woman in Arabia: The Writings of the Queen of the Desert* (Penguin Press, 2006), 21.

4 Constance Gordon Cummings, *In the Himalayas and on the Indian Plains* (Chatto and Windus, 1884), 138.

5 Janet Wallach, *Desert Queen: The Extraordinary Life of Gertrude Bell, Adventurer, Advisor to Kings, Ally of Lawrence of Arabia* (Anchor Books, 1996), 80.

6 Harriet Taylor, "Enfranchisement of Women," available at: http://www.wwhp.org/Resources/WomansRights/taylor_enfranchisement.html.

7 Taylor, "Enfranchisement."

8 Irvin Schick, "Representing Middle Eastern Women: Feminism and Colonial Discourses," *Feminist Studies* 16, no. 4 (Summer 1990), 345.

9 Gertrude Bell, *Persian Pictures* (Anthem Travel Classics, 2005), 47.

10 Antoinette Burton, *Burdens of History: British Feminists, Indian Women and Imperial Culture 1865–1915* (University of North Carolina Press, 1994), 125.

11 Burton, *Burdens of History*, 125.

12 Nupur Chaudhuri and Margaret Strobel, eds., *Western Women and Imperialism, Complicity and Resistance* (Indiana University Press, 1996), 145.

13 Burton, *Burdens of History*, 101.

14 Burton, *Burdens of History*, 104.

15 Vron Ware, *Beyond the Pale: White Women Racism and History* (Verso, 2015), 128.

16 Padma Anagol, "Feminist Inheritances and Foremothers: The Beginnings of Feminism in Modern India," *Women's History Review* 19, no. 4 (September 2010).

17 Anagol, "Feminist Inheritances," 545.

18 Kumari Jayawardena, *Feminism and Nationalism in the Third World* (Zed Books, 1986), 88.

19 Prapti Sarkar, "Swarnakumari Devi: A Forgotten Name in Bengali Literature," SheThePeople, January 23, 2020, https://www.shethepeople.tv/sepia-stories/author-swarnakumari-devi-bengali-literature/.

20 Sarkar, "Swarnakumari Devi."

21 Chaudhuri and Strobel, *Western Women and Imperialism*, 42.

22 Burton, *Burdens of History*, 54.

23 Burton, *Burdens of History*, 55.

24 Karthika Nair, "Sarojini Naidu: The Nightingale of India," Feminism in India, March 22, 2017, https://www.tandfonline.com/doi/abs/10.1080/09612025.2010.502398.

25 The Open University, "Dhanvati Rama Rau," *Making Britain: Discover How South Asians Shaped the Nation 1870–1950*, http://www.open.ac.uk/researchprojects/makingbritain/content/dhanvanthi-rama-rau.

26 Nair, "Sarojini Naidu."

Chapter Two: Is Solidarity a Lie?

1 Jeanne Madeline Weimann, *The Fair Women: The Story of the Women's Building at the World's Colombian Exposition at the Chicago World's Fair 1893* (Academy Chicago Publishers, 1981).

2 Ida B. Wells and Frederick Douglass, *The Reason Why the Colored American Is Not in the World's Columbian Exposition: The Afro-American's Contribution to Columbian Literature* (Chicago, n.p., 1893), 73.

3 Weimann, *Fair Women*, 50.

4 Barbara Ballard, "A People Without a Nation," part of the Living History of Illinois Project, http://livinghistoryofillinois.com/pdf_files/African%20Americans%20at%20the%201893%20Worlds%20Columbian%20Exposition,%20A%20People%20Without%20a%20Nation.pdf.

5 Martha Jones, "For Black Women the 19th Amendment Didn't End Their Fight for the Vote," *National Geographic*, August 2020, https://www.nationalgeographic.com/history/2020/08/black-women-continued-fighting-for-vote-after-19th-amendment/.

6 Jones, "19th Amendment."

7 Jones, "19th Amendment."

8 Jones, "19th Amendment."

9 Simone de Beauvoir, *The Second Sex* (Vintage, First Edition, 2011), 311.

10 Margaret Simons, "Beauvoir and the Problem of Racism," in *Philosophers on Race: Critical Essays,* eds. Julie Ward and Tommy Lott (Wiley-Blackwell, 2002), 260.

11 Simons, "Beauvoir."

12 de Beauvoir, *Second Sex*, 81.

13 de Beauvoir, *Second Sex*, 81.

14 Betty Friedan, "No Gods, No Goddesses," *Saturday Review*, June 14, 1975.

15 Catharine B. Stimpson, Alix Kates Shulman, and Kate Millett,

"*Sexual Politics*: Twenty Years Later," *Women's Studies Quarterly* 19, no. 3; (Fall/Winter 1991), 30.

16 Stimpson et al., "Twenty Years Later," 34.

17 Kate Millett, *Going to Iran* (Coward McCann and Geoghan, 1982), 123.

18 Millett, *Going to Iran*, 123.

19 Millett, *Going to Iran*, 92.

20 Millett, *Going to Iran,* 186.

Chapter Three: The White Savior Industrial Complex and the Ungrateful Brown Feminist

1 Anne-Marie Calves, "Empowerment: The History of a Key Concept in Contemporary Development Discourse," *Revue Tiere-Monde* 200, no. 4 (2009), 735.

2 Gita Sen and Caren Grown, *Development Crises and Alternative Visions: Third World Women's Perspectives* (Monthly Review Press, 1987), 24.

3 Sen and Grown, *Development Crises,* 24.

4 Sen and Grown, *Development Crises,* 24.

5 "Platform for Action," Fourth United Nations Conference for Women, 1995, https://www.un.org/womenwatch/daw/beijing/platform/.

6 Rafia Zakaria, "It Will Take More Than Laws to End Honor Killings in Pakistan," CNN, March 28, 2019, https://www.cnn.com/2019/03/28/opinions/pakistan-honor-killings-afzal-kohistani-zakaria/index.html.

7 Nimmi Gowrinathan, Rafia Zakaria, and Kate Cronin-Furman, "Emissaries of Empowerment," City University of New York, Colin Powell School for Civic and Global Leadership, September 2017, https://www.ccny.cuny.edu/colinpowellschool/emissaries-empowerment.

8 Zakaria, Gowrinathan, and Cronin-Furman, "Emissaries of Empowerment."

9 Ginger Ging-Dwan Boyd, "The Girl Effect: A Neoliberal Instrumentalization of Gender Equity," *Consilience* (2016), 455.

10 S. Batliwala, "Taking the Power Out of Empowerment: An Experimental Account," *Development in Practice* (2007), 557.

11 Batliwala, "Taking the Power."

12 Batliwala, "Taking the Power."

13 Rafia Zakaria, "The Myth of Empowerment," *New York Times*, October 5, 2017, https://www.nytimes.com/2017/10/05/opinion/the-myth-of-womens-empowerment.html.

14 Hanlon Joseph and Teresa Smart, "Why Bill Gates' Chickens Will Not End African Poverty," London School of Economics (blog), July 19, 2016, https://blogs.lse.ac.uk/africaatlse/2016/07/19/will-bill-gates-chickens-end-african-poverty/.

15 James Vincent, "Bolivia Rejects 'Offensive' Chicken Donation from Bill Gates," *The Verge*, June 16, 2016, https://www.theverge.com/2016/6/16/11952200/bill-gates-bolivia-chickens-refused.

16 Matthew Davies, "Bill Gates Launches Chicken Plan to help Africa Poor," BBC, June 6, 2016, https://www.bbc.com/news/world-africa-36487536.

17 Loubna Hanna Skalli, "The 'Girl Factor' and the Insecurity of Coloniality: A View from the Middle East," *Alternatives: Global, Local and Political* 40, no. 2 (2015).

18 Rod Nordland, Ash Ngu, and Fahim Abed, "How the U.S Government Misleads the Public on Afghanistan," *New York Times*, September 8, 2018.

19 Special Instructor General for Afghanistan Reconstruction, *Quarterly Report to the United States Congress*, October 30, 2016, https://www.sigar.mil/pdf/quarterlyreports/2016-10-30qr.pdf.

20 Thomas Dichter, "Is There a Foreign Aid Industrial Complex?" Medium, August 8, 2016, https://medium.com/@DichterThomas/is-there-a-foreign-aid-industrial-complex-1be4e9c03047.

21 Nick Routley, "Mapping the Global Flow of Foreign Aid," Visual Capitalist, https://www.visualcapitalist.com/mapping-the-global-flow-of-foreign-aid/.

22 Angela Bruce-Raeburn, "International Aid Has a Race Prob-

lem," DevEx, May 17, 2019, https://www.devex.com/news/opinion-international-development-has-a-race-problem-94840.

23 Corinne Gray, "Doing Good and Being Racist," *The New Humanitarian*, June 15, 2020, https://www.thenewhumanitarian.org/opinion/2020/06/15/United-Nations-racism-black-lives-matter.

24 Thalif Deen, "Survey Reveals Widespread Racism at the UN," IPS, August 21, 2020, http://www.ipsnews.net/2020/08/staff-surveys-reveal-widespread-racism-united-nations/.

25 Colum Lynch, "UN Reverses Ban on Staff Participation in Protests After Widespread Outcry," *Foreign Policy*, June 8, 2020, https://foreignpolicy.com/2020/06/08/united-nations-staff-george-floyd-protests/.

26 Routley, "Mapping the Global Flow."

27 Gita Sen, "The Changing Landscape of Feminist Organizing Since Beijing," UN Women Expert Group Meeting, Sixty-Fourth Session of the Commission on the Status of Women, September 2019, https://www.unwomen.org/-/media/headquarters/attachments/sections/csw/64/egm/sen%20gexpert%20paperdraftegmb25ep10.pdf?la=en&vs=5416.

28 Sen, "Changing Landscape."

29 Liz Ford, "US May Go Cheek by Jowl with Human Rights Abusers," *Guardian*, May 12, 2017, https://www.theguardian.com/global-development/2017/mar/13/us-cheek-by-jowl-womens-rights-abusers-gender-talks-un-commission-on-the-status-of-women-new-york.

30 UN Economic and Social Council, "Political Declaration on the Occasion of the Twenty-Fifth Anniversary of the Fourth World Conference on Women," March 2, 2020, https://undocs.org/en/E/CN.6/2020/L.1.

Chapter Four: White Feminists and Feminist Wars

1 Greg Miller, "In *Zero Dark Thirty* She Is the Hero: In Real Life the CIA Agent's Life Is More Complicated," *Washington Post*, December 10, 2012, https://www.washingtonpost.com/

world/national-security/in-zero-dark-thirty-shes-the-hero-in
-real-life-cia-agents-career-is-more-complicated/2012/12/10/
cedc227e-42dd-11e2-9648-a2c323a991d6_story.html.

2 Joana Cook, *A Woman's Place: US Counterterrorism since 9/11*
(Hurst Publishers, 2019), 66.

3 Jim Garamone, "'I Am an American Soldier Too,' Lynch to
Rescuers," American Forces Press Service, April 5, 2003,
https://www.af.mil/News/Article-Display/Article/139561/
lynch-to-rescuers-im-an-american-soldier-too/.

4 Veronique Pin-Fat and Maria Stern, "The Scripting of Private
Jessica Lynch: Biopolitics, Gender and the Feminization of
the U.S. Military," *Alternatives* 30 (2005), 25–56.

5 Cook, *A Woman's Place*, 71.

6 Pankaj Mishra, *Bland Fanatics* (Farrar Straus & Giroux, 2020).

7 Lila Abu-Lughod, *Do Muslim Women Need Saving?* (Harvard
University Press, 2013).

8 Rafia Zakaria, "Clothes and Daggers," *Aeon,* September 8,
2015,   https://aeon.co/essays/ban-the-burqa-scrap-the-sari
-why-women-s-clothing-matters.

9 George W. Bush, "Rights and Aspirations of the People of
Afghanistan," White House Archives of President George W.
Bush, https://georgewbush-whitehouse.archives.gov/infocus/
afghanistan/text/20040708.html.

10 Andrew Kramer, "Shelters Have Saved Countless Afghan
Women: So Why Are They Afraid?" *New York Times*, March
17, 2018, https://www.nytimes.com/2018/03/17/world/asia/
afghanistan-womens-shelters.html.

11 "Afghan Death Toll Hits Record High," BBC, February 24,
2019, https://www.bbc.com/news/world-asia-47347958.

12 George W. Bush, "Fact Sheet: President Bush Seeks a "Forward Strategy of Freedom: to Promote Democracy in
the Middle East," White House Archives for George W.
Bush,   https://georgewbush-whitehouse.archives.gov/news/
releases/2003/11/20031106-11.html.

13 Cook, *A Woman's Place*, 252.

14 Ahmadi Belquis and Sadaf Lakhani, "Afghan Women and Violent Extremism: Colluding, Perpetrating, or Preventing?" United States Institute of Peace, November 2016, https://www.usip.org/sites/default/files/SR396-Afghan-Women-and-Violent-Extremism.pdf.

15 Mark Mazzeti, "Vaccination Ruse Used in Pursuit of Bin Laden," *New York Times*, July 12, 2011, https://www.nytimes.com/2011/07/12/world/asia/12dna.html.

16 "Polio Eradication: The CIA and Their Unintended Victims," *Lancet* 383, no. 9932 (May 2014), https://www.thelancet.com/journals/lancet/article/PIIS0140-6736(14)60900-4/fulltext.

17 Tim McGirk, "How the Bin Laden Raid Put Vaccinators Under the Gun in Pakistan," *National Geographic*, February 2015, https://www.nationalgeographic.com/news/2015/02/150225-polio-pakistan-vaccination-virus-health/.

18 Nina Zhu, Elizabeth Allen, Anne Kearns, and Jacqueline Caglia, "Lady Health Worker Program Pakistan: Improving Access to Healthcare for Rural Women and Families," Harvard School of Public Health, May 2014, https://cdn2.sph.harvard.edu/wp-content/uploads/sites/32/2014/09/HSPH-Pakistan5.pdf.

19 Jon Boone, "Polio Vaccinator's Murder by Militants Raises Health Workers' Fears," *Guardian*, March 25, 2014, https://www.theguardian.com/society/2014/mar/25/pakistan-polio-vaccinators-murder-militants-salma-farooqi.

20 Boone, "Polio Vaccinator's Murder."

21 Srdjan Vucatic, "The Uneasy Co-Existence of Arms Trade and Feminist Foreign Policy," *The Conversation*, April 8, 2018, https://theconversation.com/the-uneasy-co-existence-of-arms-exports-and-feminist-foreign-policy-93930.

22 Vijay Prashad, "How Can Sweden Be a Peace Broker If It's Also Selling the Arms That Make the War in Yemen Possible?" *Salon*, September 4, 2019, https://www.salon.com/2019/09/04/how-can-sweden-be-a-peace-broker-for-the-war-in-yemen-if-its-also-selling-the-arms-that-make-it-possible_partner/.

23 Susanne Courtney, "Canada's Feminist Foreign Aid Pol-

icy Is Not Making Much Progress Toward a Gender Equal World," *National Post*, October 30, 2018. https://nationalpost.com/news/politics/canadas-feminist-foreign-aid-policy-isnt-making-much-progress-on-a-gender-equal-world.

24 Mersiha Gadzo, "Canadian Rights Groups Urge Trudeau to End Saudi Arms Sales," *Al Jazeera*, September 21, 2020, https://www.aljazeera.com/news/2020/9/21/canadian-rights-groups-urge-trudeau-to-end-saudi-arms-sales.

25 Leyland Cecco, "Canada Doubles Weapons Sales to Saudi Arabia Despite Moratorium," *Guardian*, June 9, 2020, https://www.theguardian.com/world/2020/jun/09/canada-doubles-weapons-sales-to-saudi-arabia-despite-moratorium.

26 Vucatic, "Uneasy Co-Existence."

27 Alissa Rubin, "A Thin Line of Defense Against Honor Killing," *New York Times*, March 3, 2015, https://www.nytimes.com/2015/03/03/world/asia/afghanistan-a-thin-line-of-defense-against-honor-killings.html.

28 "Afghan Casualties Hit Record High," UN News, February 14, 2016, https://news.un.org/en/story/2016/02/522212-afghan-casualties-hit-record-high-11000-2015-un-report.

29 Åsne Seierstad, *The Bookseller of Kabul* (Back Bay Books, 2004), xii.

30 Rod Nordland, *The Lovers: Afghanistan's Romeo and Juliet* (Harper Collins, 2016), 99.

31 Sheila Weller, *The News Sorority: Diane Sawyer, Katie Couritc, Christiane Amanpour and the (Ongoing, Imperfect, Complicated) Triumph of Women in TV News* (Penguin Books, 2015), 242.

32 Lynsey Addario, *Of Love and War* (Penguin Press, 2018).

33 Rachel Lowry, "New Study Shows Gender Disparity in Photojournalism Is Real," *Time*, September 25, 2015.

34 Lynsey Addario, It's *What I Do: A Photographer's Life of Love and War* (Penguin Books, 2016), 66.

35 https://thewire.in/media/afghan-girl-steve-mccurry-national-geographic.

36 Katherine Zoepf, "Islamic Revival in Syria Is Led by Women," *New York Times,* August 9, 2006.

37 Addario, *It's What I Do,* 54.

Chapter Five: Sexual Liberation Is Women's Empowerment

1 Kristina Gupta, "Compulsory Sexuality: An Emerging Concept," *Signs: A Feminist Journal* (Autumn 2015).

2 New York Times Review of Books, "Gloria Steinem; By the Book," November 1, 2015, https://www.nytimes.com/2015/11/01/books/review/gloria-steinem-by-the-book.html.

3 Steinem signed the Feminist Majority letter asking President Bush to "please do something" about the women in Afghanistan following 9/11.

4 Elizabeth Mesok, "Sexual Violence and the U.S.: Military Feminism, U.S. Empire and the Failure of Liberal Equality," *Feminist Studies* 42, no. 1 (2016), 2016.

5 Ahmadi Belquis and Sadaf Lakhani, "Afghan Women and Violent Extremism: Colluding, Perpetrating, or Preventing?" United States Institute of Peace, November 2016, https://www.usip.org/sites/default/files/SR396-Afghan-Women-and-Violent-Extremism.pdf.

6 Rafia Zakaria, "Women and Islamic Militancy," *Dissent* (Winter 2015), https://www.dissentmagazine.org/article/why-women-choose-isis-islamic-militancy.

7 Michael Walzer, "Debating Michael Walzer's 'Islamism and the Left,'" *Fathom* (Summer 2015), https://fathomjournal.org/debating-michael-walzers-islamism-and-the-left/.

8 Carrie Hartnett, Veronica Phifer, Danielle LaGrande, and Michaelma LeTourneau, "Advertising and Gender Roles" (1957–77) Picturing U.S. History, https://picturingamerica142762412.wordpress.com/2018/04/18/advertising-and-gender-roles-1957-1977/.

9 I am using the "wave" structure here to make the chronology easier to understand. I disagree with the use of this paradigm because it centers white and Western women and their movement as central to the history of all feminism.

10 Margalit Fox, "Helen Gurley Brown, Who Gave 'Single Girl' a Life in Full, Dies at 90," *New York Times*, August 14, 2012, https://www.nytimes.com/2012/08/14/business/media/helen-gurley-brown-who-gave-cosmopolitan-its-purr-is-dead-at-90.html.

11 Jodi Dean, "Critique or Collectivity: Communicative Capitalism and the Subject of Politics" in Digital Objects Digital Subjects, David Chandler and Christian Fuchs, eds. (University of Westminster Press, 2019), 171–182.

12 Jada Smith, "A Sex and the City for African Viewers" *New York Times*, August 14, 2016, https://www.nytimes.com/2016/08/14/fashion/an-african-city-sex-and-the-city.html.

13 Julie Turkewitz, "Bold Women, Scandalized Viewers: It's Sex and the City Senegal Style," *New York Times*, August 22, 2019, https://www.nytimes.com/2019/08/22/world/africa/senegal-mistress-of-a-married-man.html.

14 Turkewitz, "Bold Women, Scandalized Viewers."

15 Alisha Haridasani Gupta, "With Four More Shots Please! India Gets Its Own Sex and the City," *New York Times* May 6, 2020.

16 Turkewitz, "Bold Women, Scandalized Viewers."

17 Durba Mitra, *Indian Sex Lives: Sexuality and the Colonial Origins of Modern Social Thought* (Harvard University Press, 2020), 74.

18 Mitra, *Indian Sex Lives*, 73.

19 A lot more on this issue in the next chapter.

20 Mitra, *Indian Sex Lives,* 69.

21 Mitra, *Indian Sex Lives,* 100.

22 A lot more on this issue in the forthcoming chapter.

23 Raka Shome, "Global Motherhood: The Transnational Intimacies of White Femininity," *Critical Studies in Media Communication* 28, no. 5 (December 2011).

24 Shome, "Global Motherhood."

25 Treva Lindsey, "Black Women Have Consistently Been Trail-Blazers for Social Change: Why Are They So Often Relegated to the Margins?" *Time*, July 22, 2020, https://time.com/5869662/black-women-social-change/.

26 "#MeToo Movement Founder Tarana Burke Blasts Movement for Ignoring Poor Women," *Detroit Free Press*, November 15, 2018, https://www.freep.com/story/news/columnists/rochelle-riley/2018/11/15/tarana-burke-metoo-movement/2010310002/.

27 "The Problem with the 'Rainbow-Washing' of LGBTQ+Pride," *Wired*, June 21, 2018, https://www.wired.com/story/lgbtq-pride-consumerism/.

28 *Wired*, "Problem with Rainbow-Washing."

29 "Dress Coded: Black Girls, Bodies, and Bias in DC Schools," National Women's Law Center, April 2018, https://nwlc-ciw49tixgw5lbab.stackpathdns.com/wp-content/uploads/2018/04/Final_nwlc_DressCodeReport.pdf.

30 Alaa Elassar, "Muslim Athlete Disqualified from High School Volleyball Match for Wearing Hijab," CNN, September 27, 2020, https://www.cnn.com/2020/09/27/us/hijab-volleyball-disqualified-nashville-trnd/index.html.

31 Madison Carter, "Student Says Principal Forced Her to Remove Hijab and Prove Religion," ABC News, https://www.wkbw.com/news/local-news/student-says-principal-forced-her-to-remove-hijab-and-prove-religion.

32 Alaa Elassar, "Muslim Woman Arrested at Black Lives Matter Protest Forced to Remove Hijab for Mugshot," CBS News, June 25, 2020, https://cbs12.com/news/local/muslim-woman-arrested-at-black-lives-matter-protest-forced-to-remove-hijab-for-mugshot.

33 Linda Hirshman, *Get to Work . . . And Get a Life Before It's Too Late* (Penguin Random House, 2007).

34 Michaele Ferguson, "Choice Feminism and the Fear of Politics," *American Political Science Association Journal* 5, no. 1 (March 2010).

Chapter Six: Honor Killings, FGC, and White Feminist Supremacy

1 Human Rights Watch Oral Intervention at the 57th Session of the UN Commission "Violence Against Women and 'Honour'

Crimes' Item 12 - Integration of the human rights of women and the gender perspective; on Human Rights (April 6, 2001).

2 Bernard S. Cohn, *Colonialism and Its Forms of Knowledge: The British in India* (Princeton University Press, 1996), 10–11. There are parallels between the use of data and surveillance to create the colonial state and to the contemporary creation of the carceral state, which involves similar mechanisms and uses data to create sentencing guidelines that treat Black defendants differently.

3 Padma Anagol, "The Emergence of the Female Criminal in India: Infanticide and Survival Under the Raj," *History Workshop Journal* 63 (2002), 73.

4 Clare Anderson, "The British Empire 1789 to 1839," in *A Global History of Convicts and Penal Colonies* (Bloomsbury Academic Press, 2016).

5 Indian Law Commission and Thomas Macaulay, *The Indian Penal Code as Originally Intended* (1837), 272.

6 Sally Sheldon, "The Decriminalisation of Abortion: An Argument for Modernisation," *Oxford Journal of Legal Studies* 36, no. 2 (2016), 334–365.

7 D.J.R. Grey, "Gender in Late Nineteenth Century India," in *Transnational Penal Cultures: New Perspectives in Discipline, Punishment and Desistance*, eds. Vivien Miller and James Campbell (Routledge, 2018), 40.

8 D.J.R. Grey, "Gender in Late Nineteenth Century India," 43.

9 Anagol, "Emergence of the Female Criminal."

10 Anagol puts the number at four-fifths of all female prisoners.

11 Clare Anderson, *Convicts in the Indian Ocean: Transportation from South Asia to Mauritius 1815–53* (Macmillan, 2000); Anagol, "Emergence of the Female Criminal."

12 Anagol, "Emergence of the Female Criminal."

13 Margaret Arnot, "Understanding Women Committing Newborn Child Murders in Victorian England," in *Everyday Violence in Britain 1850–1950* (Longman Publishers, 2020), 55.

14 It must be noted that the crime of "female infanticide" existed as separate from infanticide in general and was used to con-

vict groups and tribal leaders to end the practice. All infanticide could have been dealt with in the same way, but the British chose not to do so.

15 Pompa Bannerjee, *Burning Women: Widows, Witches and Early Modern European Travelers to India* (Palgrave MacMillan, 2003).

16 Norberts Schurer, "The Impartial Spectator of Sati 1757–84" *Eighteenth-Century Studies* 42 No. 1 (Fall 2008).

17 Grey, "Gender in Late Nineteenth Century India," 4.

18 "Hindoo Widows," *London Magazine* 9 (December 1827), 544.

19 William Bowley, "Another Suttee Rescued," *Missionary Register*, July 1829.

20 Jules Verne, *Around the World in Eighty Days* (Createspace Independent Publishing), Chapter 12.

21 Gayatri Spivak, "Can the Sub-Altern Speak?" in *Marxism and the Interpretation of Culture*, eds. C. Nelson and J. Greenberg (Urbana: University of Illinois Press, 1988), 316.

22 Lata Mani, *Contentious Traditions: The Debate on Sati in Colonial India* (University of California Press, 1998).

23 Shakeel Anwar, "Development of Judicial System During British India," *Jagran Josh*, February 12, 2018, https://www.jagranjosh.com/general-knowledge/development-of-judicial-system-during-british-india-1518441346-1.

24 Tahir Wasti, *The Application of Islamic Criminal Law in Pakistan* (Brill Publishers, 2009), https://brill.com/view/book/9789047425724/Bej.9789004172258.i-408_013.xml.

25 Rafia Zakaria, "It Will Take More Than Laws to End Honor Killings in Pakistan," CNN, March 28, 2019, https://www.cnn.com/2019/03/28/opinions/pakistan-honor-killings-afzal-kohistani-zakaria/index.html; Nabih Bulos, "After Woman's Brutal Killing by Her Father, Jordan Asks at What Price 'Honor,'" *Los Angeles Times*, July 28, 2020, https://www.latimes.com/world-nation/story/2020-07-28/jordan-honor-killing-protests-violence-against-women; "India Struggles to Stem Rise in 'Honor Killings,'" *All Things Considered*,

NPR, July 27, 2010, https://www.npr.org/templates/story/story.php?storyId=128567642.

26 These are a general reference to the sort of cases in which honor killings occur.

27 Rothna Begum, "How to End 'Honor' Killings in Jordan," Human Rights Watch, https://www.hrw.org/news/2017/04/03/how-end-honor-killings-jordan; Raghda Obeidat, "Jordan's Struggle to Erase the Stain of Honor Crimes," News Decoder, May 22, 2019, https://news-decoder.com/honor-crimes-jordan-reform/.

28 Donna Coker, "Heat of Passion and Wife Killing: Men Who Batter/Men Who Kill," Gender Race Class Equity and Criminal Law Project (January 1992), https://www.researchgate.net/publication/314892172_Heat_of_Passion_and_Wife_Killing_Men_Who_BatterMen_Who_Kill.

29 Courtney Smith, "Who Defines 'Mutilation'? Challenging Imperialism in the Discourse on Female Genital Cutting," *Feminist Formations* (2011).

30 Smith, "Who Defines 'Mutilation'?"

31 Saida Hodzic, *The Twilight of Cutting: African Activism and Life After NGOs* (University of California Press, 2017), 104.

32 Hodzic, *The Twilight of Cutting*, 131.

33 Smith, "Who Defines 'Mutilation'?"

34 Sara Johnsdotter, "Meaning Well and Doing Harm: Compulsory Genital Examinations of Swedish African Girls," *Sexual and Reproductive Health Matters* 27, no. 2 (2019).

35 Rebecca Ratcliffe, "FGM Rates Fall from 71 Percent to 8 Percent in Africa, Study Shows," *Guardian*, November 7, 2018, https://www.theguardian.com/global-development/2018/nov/07/fgm-rates-in-east-africa-drop-20-years-study-shows.

36 "Special Agents Renew Efforts to Fight Female Genital Mutilation at Dulles Airport," ICE Press Release, June 14, 2019, https://www.ice.gov/news/releases/special-agents-renew-efforts-against-female-genital-mutilation-dulles-airport.

37 Rafia Zakaria, "Weaponized Bodies: FGM as a Pretext for

Exclusion," *Adi*, https://adimagazine.com/articles/weaponized
-bodies/.

38 Howard Goldberg PhD, et al., "Female Genital Mutila-
tion/Cutting: Updated Estimates of Women and Girls at
Risk," *Public Health Reports* 131, no. 2 (2016), 340, https://
www.ncbi.nlm.nih.gov/pmc/articles/PMC4765983/.

39 ICE, "Special Agents Renew Efforts."

40 It is unknown why the Trump administration has implemented the programs at airports instead of at nonpunitive
venues where the women and girls can actually trust those
engaging with them without fear.

41 "FBI and ICE Commended for Fighting FGM at World
Policing Awards," *Homeland Security Today*, November 21,
2019, https://www.hstoday.us/subject-matter-areas/customs
-immigration/ice-fbi-commended-at-world-policing-awards
-for-fighting-female-genital-mutilation/.

42 Independent Medical Review Team, "Executive Summary of
Medical Abuse Findings About Irwin Detention Center," Octo-
ber 21, 2020, https://www.scribd.com/document/481646674/
Executive-Summary-of-Medical-Abuse-Findings-About
-Irwin-Detention-Center/.

43 Associated Press, "US Deports Migrant Women Who Alleged
Abuse by Georgia Doctor," NBC News, November 11, 2020,
https://www.nbcnews.com/news/us-news/u-s-deports
-migrant-women-who-alleged-abuse-georgia-doctor
-n1247372.

44 Diana Gonzalez, "Forced Sterilizations: A Long and Sordid
History," March 18, 2016, American Civil Liberties Union
of Southern California, https://www.aclusocal.org/en/news/
forced-sterilizations-long-and-sordid-history.

Chapter Seven: "I Built a White Feminist Temple"

1 Audre Lorde, "The Master's Tools Will Never Dismantle the
Master's House," available at http://s18.middlebury.edu/
AMST0325A/Lorde_The_Masters_Tools.pdf.

2 Kimberlé Crenshaw, "De-Marginalizing the Intersection of Race and Sex: A Black Feminist Critique of Antidiscrimination Doctrine, Feminist Theory and Antiracist Politics," *University of Chicago Legal Forum* 1989, no. 1, https://chicagounbound.uchicago.edu/cgi/viewcontent.cgi?article=1052&context=uclf.

3 *Moore v Hugh Helicopters*, 708 F.2d 475, United States Court of Appeals of the Ninth Circuit, June 1983.

4 *Moore v Hugh Helicopters*.

5 Crenshaw, "De-Marginalizing," 140.

6 Leslie McCall, "The Complexity of Intersectionality," *Signs* 30, no. 3 (2005), 1771.

7 Christina Bose, "Intersectionality and Global Gender Equality," *Gender and Society* (January 2012), 67.

8 Momin Rahman, "Queer as Intersectionality: Theorizing Gay Muslim Identities," *Sociology* 44, no. 5 (2010), 944.

9 Crenshaw, "De-Marginalizing," 154.

10 Layla Saad, "I Built a White Feminist Temple and Now I Am Taking It Down," Layla F. Saad, November 19, 2017, http://laylafsaad.com/poetry-prose/white-feminist-temple.

Chapter Eight: From Deconstruction to Reconstruction

1 Emily Shugerman, "Don't Forget the White Women: Members Say Racism Ran Rampant at NOW," *Daily Beast*, August 12, 2020, https://www.thedailybeast.com/national-organization-for-women-members-say-racism-ran-rampant/.

2 National Organization of Women, "Structures and By-Laws," https://now.org/about/structure-and-bylaws/structure-of-now/.

3 Caroline Kitchener, "How Many Young Women Have to Cry?: Top Feminist Organizations Are Plagued by Racism, 20 Staffers Say," *Lily*, July 13, 2020, https://www.thelily.com/how-many-women-of-color-have-to-cry-top-feminist-organizations-are-plagued-by-racism-20-former-staffers-say/.

4 Kitchener, "How Many Young Women."

5 Kitchener, "How Many Young Women."

6   Kitchener, "How Many Young Women."

7   Audre Lorde, "The Uses of Anger: Women Responding to Racism," Keynote Address to the National Women's Studies Association, published in *Women's Studies Quarterly* 9, no. 3 (Fall 1981), 6–9.

8   Shugerman, "Don't Forget the White Women."

9   Abby Disney Podcast, https://www.forkfilms.com/all-ears/?event=kimberle-crenshaw.

10   "Poverty Rate by Race/Ethnicity," statistics collected by the Kaiser Family Foundation, https://www.kff.org/other/state-indicator/poverty-rate-by-raceethnicity/?currentTimeframe=0&sortModel=%7B%22colId%22:%22Location%22,%22sort%22:%22asc%22%7D.

11   "The State of Working America," Economic Policy Institute, http://www.stateofworkingamerica.org/index.html%3Fp=4193.html.

12   Robin Bleweis et al., "The Basic Facts About Women in Poverty," Fact Sheet, Center for American Progress, August 3, 2020, https://www.americanprogress.org/issues/women/reports/2020/08/03/488536/basic-facts-women-poverty/.

13   Bleweis et al., "The Basic Facts."

14   Dierdre Woods, "Invisible Women: Hunger, Poverty, Racism and Gender in the UK," Right to Food and Nutrition Watch, https://www.righttofoodandnutrition.org/files/rtfn-watch11-2019_eng-26-32.pdf.

15   "Intersecting Inequalities: The Impact of Austerity on Black and Ethnic Minority Women in the UK," Runnymede Trust, https://www.runnymedetrust.org/uploads/Executive-Summary-Intersecting-Inequalities-October-2017.pdf.

16   Nancy Fraser and Axel Honneth, *Redistribution or Recognition: A Political-Philosophical Exchange* (Verso 2003).

17   Fraser and Honneth, *Redistribution*, 18.

18   Lorde, "Uses of Anger," 6.

19   Aurielle Marie-Lucier, "Women's March on Washington: To White Women Who Were Allowed to "Resist" While We

Survived Passive Racism," *Essence*, January 23, 2017, https://www.essence.com/holidays/black-history-month/white-women-racism-womens-march-washington-privilege/.

20 Adrienne Milner, "Colour-Blind Racism and the Women's March 2017: White Feminism, Activism and Lessons for the Left," in *The Fire Now: Anti-Racist Scholarship in Times of Explicit Racist Violence* (Zed Books, 2018), 86.

21 Milner, "Colour-Blind Racism," 86.

22 Emma Kate Symons, "The Agenda for the Women's March Has Been Hijacked by Organizers Bent on Highlighting Women's Differences," *New York Times*, January 19, 2017.

23 Erin Delmore, "This Is How Women Voters Decided the 2020 Election," NBC News, November 13, 2020, https://www.nbcnews.com/know-your-value/feature/how-women-voters-decided-2020-election-ncna1247746.

24 Marisa J. Lang, "Nobody Needs Another Pink Hat: Why the Women's March Has Been Struggling for Relevance," *Washington Post*, January 12, 2020, https://www.washingtonpost.com/local/the-womens-march-sparked-a-resistance-three-years-later-its-a-movement-struggling-to-find-relevance/2020/01/11/344ccf22-3323-11ea-a053-dc6d944ba776_story.html.

25 Crenshaw, "De-Marginalizing," 154.

26 Gita Sen and Caren Grown, *Development, Crises and Alternative Visions: Third World Women's Perspectives* (Monthly Review Press, 1987), 22.

27 Nimmi Gowrinathan, Kate Cronin-Furman, and Rafia Zakaria, "Emissaries of Empowerment," *Deviarchy*, https://www.deviarchy.com/emissaries-of-empowerment/.

28 Chantal Mouffe, *For a Left Populism* (Verso 2019), 4.

Conclusion: On Fear and Futures

1 Audre Lorde, "The Master's Tools Will Never Dismantle the Master's House," available at http://s18.middlebury.edu/AMST0325A/Lorde_The_Masters_Tools.pdf.

INDEX

Abercrombie, Alexander, 124
abortion. *See* reproductive
 rights
Abu-Lughod, Lila, 84
academia, 104–5, 108–10,
 129–30, 139, 176–77
accommodation, 201
activism, 29, 39, 131–32. *See*
 also suffrage
Addario, Lynsey, 98, 99–100
Adoption Help International,
 128
affirmative change, 198
Afghanistan, 71–72, 84–85,
 94–100, 153. *See also* War
 on Terror and feminism
An African City (TV show), 120
Afridi, Shakil, 89
Ahmad, Ayn al-Hayat, 26–28
aid industrial complex, 72–73,
 89. *See also* white savior
 complex
Akroyd, Annette, 24, 25
alienation, 5–6
al-Sha'arawi, Huda, 26–28
American Association of
 University Women
 (AAUW), 181–82, 184
Amnesty International USA,
 8–9, 173, 174, 197–98
Anglobalization, 87

Anthony, Susan B., 12
anti-racism, 59
anti-rape activism, 131
appropriation, 175
arms exports, 92, 93
Around the World in Eighty Days
 (Verne), 148–49
asexuality, 108–9
austerity, 191

Bangladesh, 64–65
Barker, Kim, 95
Batliwala, Srilatha, 59, 65
Beijing 25 Conference, 76
Bell, Gertrude, 18–20, 21
Bernard, Bayle, 23
Bethune, Mary McLeod, 41–42
Bewah, Kally, 126–27
bigotry, 45–46, 54
Black Lives Matter, 74, 195,
 196
Black people, 37–38, 39,
 43–45, 225n2
Black women
 and anti-rape activism, 131
 and civil rights movement,
 43
 and de Beauvoir, 44–45, 46
 as essential workers, 195–96
 and feminist organizations,
 180–82

Black women (*continued*)
and intersectionality, 169–72
and poverty, 190
stereotypes, 127–28, 135–36
and Trump, 197
voting, 41–42
at Women's March, 194–95
World's Fair, 39
Blackburn, Helen, 29
Blair, Tony, 203–4
Bland Fanatics (Mishra), 84
Bolivia, 69
The Bookseller of Kabul (Seierstad), 95–96
Bose, Christine, 171–72
Bowley, William, 148
bravery, 99
Britain, 122–24. *See also* colonialism
British East India Company, 142
Brown, Helen Gurley, 115–16, 203
Brown, Wendy, 64
Bruce-Raeburn, Angela, 73–74
Burke, Tarana, 131
Bush, George W., 85, 86–87

Cadesky, Jessica, 93
cameos, 55
"Can the Sub-Altern Speak" (Spivak), 11–12
Canada, 92–93
capitalism
dominance of, 202–5
and empowerment, 62–65
and feminist consumers, 112–13, 114–15, 116–18
and political parties, 203–4
Sexual Politics (Millet), 114
and sexuality, 108, 133–35
See also individualism

Chambers, E. M., 126
choice feminism, 137–38
CIA, 49, 53, 110. *See also* War on Terror and feminism
cigarettes, 112–13
civil disobedience, 29. *See also* activism
civil rights movement, 43
civil-rights cases, 187–90, 191–92
class
academic settings, 105–6
Bell, 18–19
and clean stoves in India, 66
and feminist leadership, 5
and gender equality, 58
recognition/redistribution, 192–94
and white supremacy, 9
and Women's March, 195–96
Zakaria as lawyer, 187–90, 191–92
See also poverty
Clement, Marguerite, 26–28
clothing, 24–25, 64–65, 73, 75
Cocanco, Cesar, 69
Cohn, Bernard, 142
Colombia, 62
colonialism
and Austen, 12
courts, 150–51
ethnography, 142, 225n2
French Napoleonic Penal Code, 153
imperial superiority, 18–19, 20–28, 142–49
and sexual relations, 122–27
vs. suffrage, 29–31
and victim blaming, 126–27
and white privilege, 18–19, 20–22, 80

color-blindness, 10, 195, 196
Committee for Artistic and
    Intellectual Freedom,
    49–50, 52
compulsory sexuality, 107–8,
    109, 132–33, 135–36
consumerism, 112–13, 114–15,
    116–18, 134–35
Cook, Joana, 80
Cosmo Girl feminism, 116–19,
    203
Countering Violent Extremism
    (CVE), 83, 84, 88
Couric, Katie, 97
Couzins, Phoebe, 38–39
Covid-19 pandemic, 195
Crenshaw, Kimberlé, 53,
    169–72, 186, 200
criminalization, 123, 142–45,
    147
culture, 70, 156–57, 159. See
    also white savior complex

DAWN (Development Alterna-
    tives with Women in a
    New era), 57–58, 59–61
de Beauvoir, Simone, 43–47,
    54–55
deep poverty, 190
Democratic Republic of Congo,
    15–17
deportation, 164
Desai, Shivani, 183
Development Crises and Alternative
    Visions: Third World Women's
    Perspectives (Sen), 58
Dingle, Sherill, 182–84
Do Muslim Women Need Saving?
    (Abu-Lughod), 84
domestic abuse, 3–4, 5,
    140–41, 154–55, 166

double standards, 141–46,
    154–55. See also racism
Douglass, Frederick, 38, 40

East Asia, 45–46
economics, 62–66, 68–69. See
    also capitalism
ego killings, 141
Egypt, 26–28
empowerment
    co-option (overview), 201
    co-option and consumerism,
        114–15, 116–18
    co-option and economic
        focus, 62–66, 68, 76
    co-option and erasing
        politics, 60–61, 68
    co-option and queer culture,
        133–35
    co-option and recruiting
        Muslim women, 111
    core components, 201
    in India, 57–58, 59–60
    vs. power, 59
    See also sex-positive feminism
"The Enfranchisement of
    Women" (Taylor), 20
Ensler, Eve, 15–17
entrepreneurship, 68–69, 72
epistemological skepticism,
    47–48, 51, 52, 54–55, 59
erasure, 16–18, 30–31, 37–38,
    39. See also politics,
    erasure of
essential workers, 195–96
essentialization, 43–47
etiquette, 26–28
Excellent Daughters (Zoepf),
    100–102
experience, 6–8, 13–14, 201
expertise, 7–9, 13

exploitation, 95–96, 98–100
Eyben, Rosalind, 65

Farooqi, Salma, 90
Fawcett, Millicent, 29
female genital cutting (FGC),
    156–63
feminism
    and anticapitalism, 202
    discussing, 206–9
    divisions in, 4–6
    eliminating whiteness, x,
        187, 200–201, 209
    and failing feminists, 54–55
    imbalance in, 12–13
    and intersectionality, 54–55
        (see also intersectionality)
    making whiteness visible, 48,
        186–87, 200
    and perspectives from
        trauma, 8
    race and suffrage (see
        suffrage)
    serving state (see War on
        Terror and feminism)
    solidarity, 47–53, 55,
        166–67, 200–203, 209–10
    and transformational change,
        198–99
    trickle-down, 67–68, 87
    VIP feminists, 52–53
    and wave structure, 199
    women of color influencing,
        13–14
    women of color turning from,
        209–10
feminist foreign policy, 91–93
Feminist Majority Foundation
    (FMF), 181–85, 186–87
feminists/women of color
    accessing funds, 165

bonding, 57
capitalizing on friendships of,
    95–102
ceding to white feminists,
    174, 197–98, 207
class and gender equality, 58
conforming to whiteness,
    ix–x, 12, 110, 174–76,
    177–79, 186
and de Beauvoir, 43–46
disadvantages against men, 10
and experiences/stories, 6–8,
    13–14, 201
as failing, 155
India 1800s, 25–26
in Iran, 49–54, 55
leadership roles, 74–75
and men of color, 11, 58, 75,
    83
as oppressed, 18–19, 20–24,
    66–67, 70
pitfalls, 207, 208
and poverty, 190–92, 193–94
recognition (see recognition)
and resources, 5
roles in white feminism, 55
and sexuality, 135–36
showing gratitude, 28
texts in academia, 130
turning from feminism,
    209–10
and voting, 41–42 (see also
    suffrage)
white feminists using, 32–36,
    41, 177–78
and white intersectionalists, ix
and white women taking
    charge, 51–54, 55, 197–98
and Women's March, 194–96
See also specific women/
    countries

feminized imperialism, 24. *See also* imperial superiority
Ferguson, Niall, 87
fetishization, 33–36, 40–41
first-wave feminism. *See* suffrage
forced hysterectomies, 163–65
Fortson-Washington, China, 180–81, 186
Four More Shots Please (TV show), 121
Fraser, Nancy, 192–93, 198
Freeland, Chrystia, 92
French Napoleonic Penal Code, 153
Friedan, Betty, 47

Gates Foundation Chicken Program, 17, 68–69
gender equality, 58, 97. *See also* War on Terror and feminism
genital exams, 124, 125
Ghana, 120, 158
Ghani, Rula, 71–72
"Global Bazaar," 32–36, 41
Goldberg, Michelle, 133
gratitude, 28
Guatemala, 128
Gupta, Kristina, 107

headscarves, 11, 49–51, 136, 177
Her Honor (Quraishi), 129
heteronormativity, 107–8, 124
Hills, Rachel, 133
Hindu women, 122, 124, 145–49. *See also* India
Hispanic women, 180–81, 188, 190, 191–92
Hodzic, Saida, 157–58

Hong Kong, 125
honor killings
    assumptions, 141
    as colonial interventions, 150–51
    definition, 140–41
    and education, 61
    Jordan laws, 153–54
    and Qisas and Diyat Ordinance, 151–52
    and Western domestic abuse, 154–55
    Zakaria's talk, 177–79
Hossain, Begum Rokeya Sakhawat, 26
hysterectomies, 163–65

ignorance of global south. *See* white savior complex
Immigration and Customs Enforcement (ICE), 160–64
imperial superiority, 18–19, 20–28, 45–46, 51–52, 142–45. *See also* white savior complex
imperialism. *See* feminized imperialism; imperial superiority
Imperialism and Its Forms of Knowledge (Cohn), 142
India
    Bewah murder, 126–27
    British abortion/infanticide laws, 142–45, 225n14
    British Common Law, 150–51
    British ethnography, 142
    clean stoves initiative, 56–57, 64, 66–67
    DAWN and empowerment, 59–61, 65–66

India (*continued*)
  feminism vs. colonialism,
    29–31
  sati, 145–49
  and sexual relations, 121,
    122, 123–27
  suffragists white savior
    complexes, 23, 24–26,
    29–31, 45
individualism, 103, 118–19,
    168–69, 173, 202–3
inequality of wealth, 73–74. *See
    also* poverty
infanticide, 142–45, 225n14
*Inside Gender Jihad: Women's
    Reform in Islam* (Wadud),
    129–30
international development. *See*
    white savior complex
"International Development Has
    a Race Problem"
    (Bruce-Raeburn), 73–74
International Women's Day,
    49–50
intersectionality
  about, 169–72
  and ceding space, ix
  and de Beauvoir, 43–46
  definition, ix, 170
  and feminist history, 54–55
  and LGBTQI, 135
  and Millett in Iran, 53–54
  and transformational change,
    198–99
  and Women's March, 195
Iran, 49–54, 55
Iraq. *See* War on Terror and
    feminism
Irwin County Detention Center
    (ICDC), 163–65
Islamic law, 129–30, 150–51

Islamophobia, 111
It's What I Do (Addario), 98

Jewish people, 44–45
Johnsdotter, Sara, 159–60
Jordan, 153–54
journalists, 152–53

Kaplan, Robert, 84
Kier, Sophie, 49
Ku Klux Klan, 42

Labor of Love (Weigel), 117
Lady Health Worker Program,
    90–91
Latina women, 128, 164
Lebanon, 101
legitimacy, 9
LGBTQI people, 108, 122,
    133–35, 194
Lindsay, Treva, 131
Lorde, Audre, 168, 185–86,
    193–94, 209
Of Love & War (Addario), 98
Lucier, Aurielle Marie, 194
Lynch, Jessica, 81–82

Martin, Tess, 186
McCall, Leslie, 171
McCurry, Steven, 99–100
Memphis riots, 131
men
  of color, 11, 22, 58, 75, 83
  and mainstream feminism,
    10
  "Sultana's Dream" (Hossain),
    26
  white savior complex, 11, 22,
    75
#MeToo movement, 131–32
microloans/credits, 64, 65

Millett, Kate, 47–55, 113–15
Mishra, Pankaj, 84
misogyny, 82
Mistress of a Married Man (TV show), 121
modernization, 157–58
monogamy, 122–23
Moore v Hughes Helicopter, 169–70
moral inferiority, 126–29, 135–36, 142–49, 156
Morris, Jane Mosbacher, 88
mothers, 126–29
Mozambique, 69
Muslim women
    and headscarves, 11, 49–51, 136, 177
    and sex, 106–7, 110
    and white feminist ideas, 110
    Zakaria's graduate paper, 129–30
    See also Afghanistan; honor killings; War on Terror and feminism
My Life on the Road (Steinem), 110

Naidu, Sarojini, 29
names, 176
Namibia, 125
Napier-Moore, Rebecca, 65
National Organization of Women (NOW), 85, 180–82, 184–85, 186–87
National Women's Studies Association (NWSA), 185–86, 193–94
Native American women, 128, 190
neoimperialism. *See* white savior complex

neoliberalism, 64, 203–4. *See also* capitalism
NGOs (Non-governmental organizations), 62–63, 72–74, 76, 158–59, 204. *See also* international development
nonmonogamy, 122. *See also* sex-positive feminism
Nordland, Rod, 97

objectivity, 7–8
Operation Limelight, 160–63
othering
    de Beauvoir, 43–46
    domestic abuse, 154–55
    "Global Bazaar," 33–36, 41
    at Manhattan wine bar, 1–2, 4, 6
    and others' oppression, 11–12, 55 (*see also* imperial superiority)
    vs. solidarity, 202
    stories vs. power, 6–9
    and white savior complexes, 16
    World's Columbian Exposition, 40
    Zakaria's honor killings talk, 177–79

Pakistan, 61, 89–90, 105–6, 129, 151–52. *See also* War on Terror and feminism
Palmer, Bertha, 38–39
patriarchy
    and sati, 149
    Sexual Politics (Millet), 47, 113–14
    and state, 79
    and white women, 172–73

patriarchy (*continued*)
  World's Columbian Exposi-
    tion, 40
performing
  and alcohol, 1–2
  editing stories, 4, 9–10
  "Global Bazaar," 34–35
  and sexual openness, 107–8,
    109, 132–33, 135–36
  wokeness, 175–76
Persian Pictures (Bell), 21
philosophy, 43–44
photographs, 98, 99–101
plastic surgery, 156–57
police, 3
politics, erasure of
  overview, 13, 202–5
  Afghan women, 88–89
  British suffragists, 23
  Canadian feminist foreign
    policy, 93
  international development,
    60–63, 68, 70, 76
  and sacrifice in feminism,
    137–38
poverty, 62–63, 70, 187,
  190–92. *See also* white
  savior complex
Powar, Soonderbai, 25
power
  in academia, 177
  of aid industrial complex,
    73–74
  capitalism and feminism,
    118–19
  vs. empowerment, 59
  vs. livelihoods, 201
  and othering, 6–9, 36
  through privilege, 19, 51, 52,
    53
  and traditional ways, 57

white feminists' positions,
  6–8, 176
precarity, 105–6
Preventing Violent Extremism
  (PVE), 88
Pride festivals, 134
PROMOTE, 71–72
prostitution, 123–25
publishing, 25

Qazi courts, 150, 151, 152
Qisas and Diyat Ordinance,
  151–52
Quit India Movement, 29
Quraishi, Asifa, 129

racialized wealth, 73–74
racism
  and aid industrial complex,
    73–74
  compulsory genital exams,
    159–60, 162, 163
  and epistemological skepti-
    cism, 54
  and equality in professional
    spaces, 58
  and feminist organizations,
    180–86, 194–95
  and recognition, 171
  recognizing, 207
  and suffrage, 20–23, 29
  and United Nations, 74
  World's Columbian Exposi-
    tion, 40–41
  See also colonialism; double
    standards
radical politics. *See* activism;
  Millett, Kate
Rahman, Momin, 172
rainbow-washing, 133–35
Ramabai, Pandita, 25

Rau, Dhanvanthi Rama, 29
reactionary stances, 206–8
rebellion vs. resilience,
    10–11
recognition, 11, 52–53, 171,
    192–93, 199
redistribution, 192–94, 199
Redistribution or Recognition
    (Fraser), 192
relatability, 7–8, 11
reproductive rights, 76,
    126–27, 142–43
resources, 5
reverse racism, 195
*Revolution from Within: A Book of
    Self- Esteem* (Steinem), 119
Rich, Adrienne, 107
Rubin, Alissa, 94

Saad, Layla, 174–75
sati, 145–49
Satthianadhan, Krupabai, 25
Saudi Arabia, 92, 93, 100–101
Save the Children, 89, 91
The Second Sex (de Beauvoir),
    43–45
second-wave feminism,
    112–15, 118
securo-feminism, 84, 86–88.
    See also War on Terror and
    feminism
Seierstad, Åsne, 95–96
self-preservation, 174
Sen, Gita, 57–60, 75–76
Senegal, 121, 156–57
sex, 48
Sex and the City (TV show),
    119–21, 136
Sex and the Single Girl (Brown),
    115
sex-positive feminism

and academia, 104–5,
    108–10
and choice feminism, 138
and colonial history, 122–27,
    142–45
and consumerism, 112–13,
    114–15, 132–33
and corporate friendly
    working-girls, 115–19
as "discovered" by white
    women, 120–22
in India, 122
and intersectionality, 135
and performance, 107–8,
    109, 132–33
Sexual Revolution, 112–15
television shows, 119–21
Zakaria's graduate paper,
    129–30
Sexual Politics (Millet), 47–48,
    113–14
sexuosociety, 108, 134. *See also*
    compulsory sexuality
Shah of Iran, 49–50
shelters, 5, 85–86, 94
"Shelters Have Saved Countless
    Afghan Women." (article),
    85–86
Shook, Teresa, 194
Shulman, Alix, 47
slavery, 46
Smeal, Eleanor, 85, 182–84, 185
Smith, Courtney, 156, 159–60
solidarity, 200–203, 209–10
Southborough Franchise
    Committee, 30
Spivak, Gayatri Chakravorty,
    11–12, 74–75, 149
state, 79. *See also* War on Terror
    and feminism
Steinem, Gloria, 52–53, 110

stereotypes, 44, 46, 127–28
Stopes, Charlotte Carmichael,
   29
stoves, 56–57, 64, 66–67
subaltern, 11–12
suffrage
   vs. battling colonialism,
      29–31
   and Bell, 19–20
   celebrating, 42–43
   and racism, 20–26, 28–29
   and Truth, 170–71
   World's Columbian Exposi-
      tion, 36–39
"Sultana's Dream" (Hossain), 26
Sweden, 91–92, 159–60
Symons, Emma Kate, 195
Syria, 101–2

The Taliban Shuffle (Barker), 95
Taylor, Harriet, 20
technocratic solutions, 204–5
third-wave feminism, 115
Todd, Bridget, 194–95
tokenism, 174, 182
torture, 77–79
transformational change,
   198–99, 206, 208–9
transgender people, 122, 194.
   See also LGBTQI people
trauma
   aversion to, 5–6
   and civil-rights cases, 189
   stories of, 8, 15–16, 55, 178,
      189
Trump, Donald, 76, 156, 183,
   196–97
Truth, Sojourner, 170–71

UN Global Alliance for Clean
   Stoves, 56–57

United Nations, 64, 66–67, 74.
   See also various organiza-
   tions/initiatives
universalization, ix, 172–73,
   175, 195, 200
U.S. Aid and International
   Development Agency
   (USAID), 71–72

vaccinations, 89–91
value, 63–64
Van Pelt, Toni, 181, 182, 185
veiling. See headscarves
Verne, Jules, 148–49
victim blaming, 126–27
violence against women, 94. See
   also domestic abuse
virtue signalling, 17–18, 93. See
   also white savior complex
voting, 41–42. See also suffrage

Wadud, Amina, 129–30
Wallström, Margot, 91–92
Walzer, Michael, 111–12
War on Terror and feminism
   overview, 79–81
   double agents, 82–83, 88–91
   doublespeak, 91–93
   and female soldiers, 81–82
   and female torturers, 77–79
   Feminist Majority Founda-
      tion, 182
   journalists, 94–102
   Muslim women implicated,
      110–11
   and Steinem, 110
   white savior complex, 82,
      83–88, 95
Weeks, Monica, 180–81, 186
Weigel, Moira, 117
Wells, Ida B., 38, 39

West-centric ideas
　de Beauvoir on Asia, 45–46
　equality in professional
　　spaces, 58–59
　individual as entrepreneur,
　　68–69
　and Iraqi women's rights,
　　87
　Millett in Iran, 51–54
　sexual liberation seminar,
　　109
　trade, 64–65
　See also othering; white savior
　　complex
Whiskey Tango Foxtrot (film),
　94–95
white feminists
　de Beauvoir's othering, 43–46
　as defacto feminism, 55
　definition, ix
　Millett in Iran, 51–55
　and positions of power, 6–8
　recognizing feminists of color
　　(see recognition)
　taking charge, 51–54, 55,
　　197–98
　unintentional whiteness, 11
　values, 95
　and wave structure, 199–200
　vs. whiteness, 200, 207–8
　See also suffrage
white fragility, 26–28, 199
white men, 11, 22, 58, 75
white privilege
　and choice, 138
　and colonialism, 18–19,
　　20–22, 80
　and colorblind feminism, 10
　examining, 172
　feminist organizations,
　　183–84

Millett in Iran, 51–55
and self-made mythology,
　168–69, 173
white savior complex
　adoption of babies of color,
　　128
　aid industrial complex
　　overview, 72–73
　chicken entrepreneurship,
　　68–69
　in classroom, 176–77
　clean stoves in India, 56–57,
　　64, 66–67
　consultations, 39, 66, 69, 71,
　　162
　dismissing political agitation
　　(see politics, erasure of)
　as distraction/cover-up, 65,
　　70–71, 75
　economic empowerment,
　　62–66, 68–69
　erasing people of color,
　　16–18
　and FGC, 158–59, 160–62
　and gratitude, 28
　PROMOTE in Afghanistan,
　　71–72
　racism, 73–74
　and sati, 148
　shelter systems, 5
　War on Terror and feminism,
　　82, 83–88, 95
　and white goals, 58
　white men vs. men of color,
　　11, 75, 83
　See also imperial superiority;
　　suffrage; West-centric
　　ideas
white-supremacist hierarchy, 80
white supremacy, 9, 12–13,
　196–97, 208

whiteness
  centering, 15–18, 23, 26–27,
    51–52, 175
  expelling, x, 187, 200–201,
    209
  exposing for solidarity, 48,
    186–87, 200
  and imbalance in feminism,
    12–13
  of NGOs, 73–74
  and term "woman," 54
  and trauma, 6
  as unintentional, 11
  and white feminism, ix
  vs. white feminists, 200,
    207–8
  and white supremacy, 208
  and womanhood intersec-
    tion, 172–74
"Who Defines 'Mutilation'?"
  (Smith), 156
wokeness, 175–76
A Woman's Place: US Counterterrorism Since 9/11 (Cook),
  80
"Women and Islamic Militancy"
  (Zakaria), 111–12
"Women Left for Dead— And
  the Man Who's Saving
  Them" (Ensler), 15–17
women of color. See feminists/
  women of color
Women's Caucus of the Indiana
  General Assembly, 177–79
Women's Indian Association,
  29–30
Women's March, 194–96, 197

women's shelters, 5, 85–86, 94
World Bank, 62–63, 65
World's Columbian Exposition,
  36–41

Yemen, 92, 93

Zakaria, Rafia
  about, 2–4
  at Amnesty International
    USA, 173, 174, 197–98
  compulsory sexuality article,
    132–33
  domestic abuse, 140
  and feminist art fair, 32–36,
    41
  goal of book, 206–10
  graduate school paper,
    129–30, 139
  as lawyer, 187–90, 191–92
  Manhattan wine bar, 1–2,
    9–10
  rejecting feminist waves, 199
  sexual liberation seminar,
    104–7, 108–10
  and truth about hardships,
    6–7, 9–10
  "Women and Islamic
    Militancy," 111–12
  women in family, 10–11
  Women's Caucus of the
    Indiana General Assembly,
    177–79
zenana visits, 21
Zero Dark Thirty (film), 77–79,
  91
Zoepf, Katherine, 100–102